Nassim Nakad was born in Lebanon in 1975. He grew up in the exact neighbourhood where the long civil war started. He went from photography to taking filming courses in Italy and Canada. He has worked as a TV series editor, videographer and documentary maker. It wasn't long before, time and passion took him back to the oldest form of storytelling 'writing'.

The book is a collection of real stories which have been mostly lived or told by those who lived them; there's nothing to be thankful about other than life itself and the pure coincidence of staying alive.

Nassim Nakad

WAR TRAUMA CHRONICLES

AUSTIN MACAULEY PUBLISHERS™

LONDON • CAMBRIDGE • NEW YORK • SHARJAH

A CIP catalogue record for this title is available from the British Library.

ISBN 9781035802517 (Paperback)
ISBN 9781035802524 (ePub e-book)

www.austinmacauley.com

First Published 2024
Austin Macauley Publishers Ltd®
1 Canada Square
Canary Wharf
London
E14 5AA

I would like to thank my family and friends who always supported me through my journey, no matter which road I took.

Table of Contents

War Traumas

Here comes another story; another struggle to find the start; another search for that specific moment that initiated a series of events that led to a snowball effect, a cocktail mixed with 'lost childhoods, war traumas, images of explosions, shattered buildings, cars, dead bodies and tales of broken hearts'.

I'm trying to write about memories that I couldn't erase, no matter how hard I tried. Traumas, paranoia, schizophrenia, phobias amongst other mental diseases are inscribed and inherited in our DNA. Unfortunately, I'm passing it down to my offspring.

But why? Why do I contribute to this madness after all these tragic experiences?

Why do humans still reproduce at all?

Didn't anyone learn anything at all after all these incidents we caused? The effects we left on Planet Earth and the universe?

The devastating harm we did happened in a fraction of a millisecond of our societies' lifespan.

The blame game, the God's guilt complex, the infinite search for an elixir of life and the eternal afterlife dream…

Why did I fall for these traps? Was it really traumatising?

Was it a nightmare or an illusion? Is time a real healer?

Do traumas fade away like old memories?

Unfortunately, I could never answer those questions, and maybe by telling others about my story, I'll be able to find peace one day.

Where and when to start my story from? What was the first memory?

Which memory wrote the first line?

Well, I was born in the era of the Cold War, in a warzone, in the Middle-East, where the fight of giants was played in the backyard of fools.

Obviously, that could be a good start especially that my mom was taken to the hospital in tanks and military trucks on multiple occasions for false alarms caused by my hard karate baby kicks.

A civil war had started just a month earlier, initiated by a few guys opening fire at a bus carrying refugees.

Some say they were innocent people and other say there were armed militants hiding in that bus…

It doesn't really matter and only simple-minded people would believe historians and their stories.

The irony is that only after I wrote the title and the first paragraph of my story that I met an old man refusing to age.

After a long day at the beach, lots of booze was making everybody a little hyper, loud and playful…The sun was setting and the smartest drunken decision was to continue drinking in a little cosy chalet…

Amidst a group of the vain younger guys and girls of our social media era, modernised with their toned bodies, tan skins and empty heads, the old man was entertaining the crowd while probably having nostalgia about his own long gone youth…

For an unknown reason, I preferred the company of the wiser man. I started a conversation about the vanity of this generation, its shameless behaviours and how there's no more values…It was a little hypocritical though, because in that current state, I wouldn't be considered any better, blending well with the younger entourage.

I don't know why but the conversation shifted to the start of the war. It spontaneously happened without any prior intention.

I was getting a beer from the fridge and I stopped for a chat; he sipped his cold aged whiskey with no ice and told me how life is changing, how virtues of yesterday became the iniquities of today…He paused for a second and said,

"Maybe it was the war that changed everything," and then he paused again as if he was checking his own words and continued, "or maybe it's a natural change with time."

I didn't have much to add, except to confirm that we are living in a declining period of civilisation.

"It must be the globalisation that is causing this deterioration in virtues."

Out of the blue, he told me how he shot that famous 'war-initiating bus' with two other men…

He gave me 'his' side of the story, and of course, he explained the motives behind the heroic action that saved the country from disappearing from the map.

He even went further to say he has no regrets; the dead body of a young girl that he found between the corpses was the only thing that made him feel remorse and cry like a child.

However, that didn't change his mind about his actions. He just hated them more and blamed them for killing that angel by putting her on that bus…I'm not a historian and I have no interest in finding out the truth, because nothing is true and nothing is right.

I just knew then the undeniable reason why I was taken to hospital under heavy bombing over and over again…

However, those stories are way before my recorded memories.

Even though I kicked like a mule and was part of the events that followed for many years, I never had any contribution in shaping those stories.

The bombs, the death and the hatred that surrounded my every day's existence since the eight months in my mom's womb were of an enormous effect…However, in those first few years of my life, I wouldn't recall that special sparkle that created what will become the person I am or the story that I'm about to tell.

The Start

It all started when I was six years old. I was living in the worst neighbourhood in a little country called Lebanon; in the same street that a civil war started and divided the country into two sides, east and west, Christian and Muslim, Soviet Union allies and American allies…or that's what we were told.

My daily route to school was a way paved with snipers, containers and sandbags dividing the two sides.

Few people would dare cross that street; most would avoid it by taking a longer road.

The story began on a sunny cold autumn morning. As usual, I waited with my younger cousin 'Mich' on the building's gate for our ride to come pick us up and drop us at school.

Our peach jam sandwiches in our hands, the kind of jam made at home from local seasonal fruits and lots of love. It was in the times when love was still considered more important than organic…I can still remember that taste to this day.

We had backpacks full of useless heavy books that taught us how to conform to a small group of *Homo sapiens*; the alphabet, mathematics and a bunch of other materials that increased our self-confidence instead of our respect for Mother Nature.

It wasn't only us though, nobody knows at what point in humanity's evolution the brain got suddenly bigger, allowing our ancestors to start imagining complex equations, recognising time and planning the future. It's a missing link that neither Darwin nor our DNA can answer.

Some say it was a miracle, a blessing that led us to the level of our present civilisation.

Others say it was Mother Nature's adaptation and evolution process. Some even say that it might have been a genetic manipulation by an advanced alien civilisation.

For me, it was just a nasty joke in the history of the universe.

It's definitely more than a coincidence, more than an accident or a bang.

One thing is for sure, it's at that point of history, that humans started thinking that they were so special, created in the image of God, rulers of the world and the centre of the universe…

Even when the sciences advanced and physicists started uncovering some of the basic ingredients and theories of our existence, the symptoms were getting worse and people kept on getting more delusional and arrogant.

My group was no different, we were taught that we were Phoenicians. That we invented the alphabet and took the world out of the dark ages into literacy…They overloaded us with useless information and details of unproved records that filled our books and later our heads.

Going back to that day, my cousin and I reached the school, and before we entered the gate, my younger cousin realised that he forgot to pick up his backpack from the floor, he started crying, knowing that the teacher won't be happy with him coming to class without any books.

It only took him a few seconds of crying for me to look at him and tell him not to worry because I knew the way home. I told him that we can easily walk back, get his bag and come back to school in no time.

It actually sounded like lots of fun for both of us, better than sitting in a class and day dreaming of greater places.

I was confident back then, even though to this day, I still consider myself bad at directions, and without a GPS, I'd rarely reach my destination.

At six years old, I knew the shortest way back home, but as I already mentioned, the street wasn't the safest. It was more like the snipers' practice zone, the desperate, rushed, careless or suicidal people's street.

It was in that same street, two years later, that my other, 20 something years old cousin 'Sam', who used to take me to the merry-go-round, get me candies and play a major role in my personal escape of the ugly reality of daily war, had a fatal accident.

It was in that same street that a young unarmed man crossed on his little newly purchased Vespa scooter, as fast as he can to avoid being noticed, with a rated speed of 60 km/h…

But on the other side of that street, in a destroyed building, in some apartment, behind the containers and the sandbags, there was a sniper…maybe smoking a cigarette, having a drink or just waiting for some fun…No one could tell what really happened, but the trigger was pulled, one shot…

At that moment, a bullet travelled in space and time with an approximate speed of 650 metres per second. My cousin

Sam must have heard it first and didn't know if he should stop or go faster, he had less than two seconds before the bullet reached him.

There was no chance for a smart reaction, it was all due to luck…The sniper was hoping for a bull's-eye and my cousin was hoping for a home run.

The odds were equal, but all possibilities were on the table, the bullet entered the scared unarmed man's lower part. From his back it went through his kidney and then found its way out…The scooter kept going the few metres to the safe side, but when it stopped, it was too late. The sniper won.

If they were in a casino, we would have seen the sniper jumping from joy and some people cheering for his win, maybe an exotic gold digger stripper would have been making a move and getting close to him, the waitresses would be bringing him his drinks expecting a big drunken generous tip…

While the other gambler, 'Sam, would have been cussing his loss, trying to stay calm, cool and composed but with no success…In fact, no financial loss could be greater than the loss of his existence.

The sniper didn't win a big prize cash to get him a better life, even though, I'm sure he did celebrate one way or another, maybe even got some smiles and cheers for his achievement.

I never got over the pain of losing a caring soul, an idol…

I felt grief and surprised at the amount of misery one bullet can bring. However, on the long term this tragedy affected me in a different way…it made me wonder about the human nature, faith and God.

It made me think back to that day, as my cousin and I walked back home, multiple possible scenarios crossed my mind:

1. The sniper was still sleeping, after all it was too early and snipers don't have obligations to wake up that early.
2. The sniper was having his first cigarette with a coffee, and he didn't bother to stop in order to shoot two young boys.
3. We were too young and the sniper's conscience didn't allow him to pull the trigger, even though I doubt that people fighting wars have any conscience.
4. Slow targets were too easy for him and he decided to spare us, save the bullet.
5. He thought about it for a second then decided to postpone it for another time when we get bicycles, scooters or motorbikes…It would be more challenging and he would enjoy it more.
6. Was it the same sniper who took pleasure in shooting a harmless young man on a scooter that let two kids pass safely?
7. Was it a supernatural intervention that prevented him from taking a shot or two?
8. Was it my guardian angel who blinded the sniper and maybe a couple of his friends?

I still have no answers, and those questions still haunt me every now and again.

I sometimes consider the probability that I'm dead in all parallel universes and this is the only version of me lucky enough to cheat death.

However, luck is overrated, and it makes lots of sense since we consider life a gift and not an ever-ending prison sentence?

Anyhow, I'm not writing this story to judge or justify our regularly changing values and virtues as they are depicted by our society.

So, I'll just travel back in time to that six-year-old boy spared by a sniper, walking slow few kilometres, enjoying the cool air on his cheeks and ignoring the smell of death and fear…

I clearly recall that day; the 'nonchalance' of our actions, the pleasure of our slow walk and the innocence of our conversation. It must have taken us so long but we reached the building, took my cousin's backpack and went straight back to school.

Thinking about it right now, I wonder how none of the people stopped us to ask why we were walking all alone or if there was something wrong…

My only rational explanation would be: 'war must have kept those grown-ups so busy with their own survival plans, and their old realistic version of the living dead'.

Once the backpack was collected, there was the second half of the mission: 'Walking back to school'.

I must have been instinctually a gambler, because I took the longer safer road on the way back…

I'm not sure if I realised the danger, we were in. Neither me nor Mich seemed to be worried about safety and security at that time, but I didn't take the same risk twice.

Time goes by slowly when you're young! In fact, every second feels like a lifetime that reaches into eternity.

It doesn't matter how short or long that next second would be, or if it's the last one or not…there would still be a story to tell and something to be said.

Our little adventurous walk came to an end and we made it back to school right after the first break. The two kilometres' road took us about a little more than two hours and a half.

We were back to school and in our playground, I looked at 'Mich', we exchanged some satisfactory glances and smiles about a morning well spent, I dropped him at the door of his classroom, said bye and went straight to my class.

I entered the classroom expecting a trophy, but instead, my teacher slapped me across the face for being late.

To my surprise, she didn't even ask about the reason of my tardiness. I never got grounded or reported to my parents…Maybe that teacher thought I was having a walk in an imaginary park.

Too bad I don't remember her name or anything else about her, so she'll always be Miss Evil to me or to be more precise 'a harmless Miss Parasite'. I took that slap like a big boy, I shed no tears and felt no remorse, but there was a strange sadness deep inside of me, something that went beyond losing my faith in teachers and the educational system. It was…as if I realised that two years later an emotional pain will happen on that same street and a harder lesson would be learned, harder than a slap, a punch or a random physical pain.

I learned that what doesn't kill you only makes you stronger. I learned that mortars, unlike bullets, travel slower than the speed of sound. I learned that a car explosion would be heard by the victims, even if they died on the spot.

While we were going to school, the 'grown-ups' men were collecting all related information from the battlefield; I've heard of street fighters who bragged about avoiding the mortars by jumping or ducking down just before it hits the land while others were too slow or less focussed to react that fast, they either lost their lives or goy injured by flying fragments.

I learned that war is not a fun game, that there were no second chances and there was nothing to prove…And still, an entire nation wanted to play.

No matter how much my stories were important to me, they were insignificant to the events happening around me. The war was at its peak and while I was playing the good/bad cop at school, there was much more going on beyond the scope of my understanding. Mortars and explosions were collecting bodies and souls. Many years later I learned important facts about mortar's impact on that little war I lived as a child.… undeniable fact is that it's not as much as luck or a coincidence that would kill a person as much as it can be nonchalance or ignorance. Well, to quote facts as I heard it from a close war survivor, "a witness of war events", a personal security guard of a high politician" and "a War Hero". He explained to me how mortars were as lethal and effective in that war as Jupiter's thunderbolt. That man told me the stories that I was not aware were happening either while I was playing at school, hiding in shelters or dreaming of a better life. Those stories felt so real as if I was there. For me, when he was narrating his stories, he resembled Jupiter in its glory, but to many others that knew him and listened to him, he was labelled as a crouching tiger, thunder man or just a leading hero.

Interestingly, Jupiter is by far the largest planet in our solar system, its powerful gravity helps protect earth from incoming debris; some astronomers believe that we exist only because of our big brother Jupiter; he's our shield and protection from comets and repeated extinctions.

In a way, Jupiter was and is a hero; the gods and the planets are mixed like rum and coke; humans on the other side are the little pinch of lime.

Let me get back to my story though, that Jupiter that I'd call hero once told me, "You know, I feel so lucky and grateful that I'm still alive."

I said, "You are lucky that you survived the war, but many did not." After a short pause, I said, "Is it called luck or a coincidence?"

He smiled to me and answered, "Let me tell you about mortars. You know, in the middle of a silent night, a soldier could hear the mortar's launch, and its hum as it flies towards its target and finally, its landing. Few seconds and how quick your reaction, are what could determine if you live, get injured or die."

As a war hero once told me, "It's funny how people are labelled a hero for different reasons." Apparently, my reason was that he spared me of becoming an orphan at a very young age.

He continued "I was very young and I think God always was on my side."

I said, "But you were in a war killing other people."

Hero said, "I only killed people that deserved to die... I was acting on self-defence and we had no choice."

I said, "Yeah, okay, but God doesn't take sides."

"Let me tell you a story," he said. "This one night, very quiet, unusually quiet, not even one sniper breaking the silence of devilish hell."

I didn't want to interrupt with my sarcastic comments so I just shook my head, and he continued, "Your dad asked me to go check what was so bizarre about that night…so we went for a walk."

Suddenly, the suspense of the story consumed me and gave him my full attention.

Hero said, "We started walking, on the frontier's lines and an army soldier was hiding behind a stack of sandbags.

We asked him: "what's the story, right?"

He replied: "it's crazy, I can hear the mosquitoes…"

There was a short pause as if to recall the exact words, then he continued, "I heard something coming from far and I screamed duck down. Next thing I see was the army soldier dead on the floor with your dad pushing against his chest or heart and saying: "I'm bleeding".

"What the fuck!" I exclaimed.

Hero continued, "It's the divine intervention, I stood up and carried him to an emergency r, the ricochet went through his chest but didn't kill him. Unlike many other militants, he survived."

I didn't know what to say but the mortars stories didn't finish there, he continued narrating about many other occasions and the 'Divine Intervention'. He described to me how he felt his hands and his body reacting multiple times in order to save him and some of his co-militants.

The repetition of those events were becoming exaggerated as a fairy tale, but then he paused for a bit as if he was trying to prove a point.

Hero then said: "Many years later on a heavily bombarded frontier, I had few guys with me and I was getting cocky about my skills. As usual, I heard the launch of a mortar and I shouted duck down as I always did…all four of us were on the floor and I heard the landing nearby, I stood up laughing and said it's a malfunctioning one."

I smiled and then he continued with even a louder laugh from the heart.

Hero continued, "The mortar then exploded and a tiny ricochet hit my brain and got stuck in a vein, blood started dripping and I felt the heat of it. Later on, I realised that French mortars had a delayed few seconds before they explode."

He laughed as if it was a nasty joke played on him. He survived the ricochet with that tiny piece still stuck in his head. He couldn't confirm any 'Divine Intervention' but he proved a point: 'a person only dies when it's their time to die'.

I laughed with him and thought of those who died walking on the streets or even sleeping in their beds.

Playing War Games

My early youth memories were split between the school playground and the neighbourhood's daily life.

It was a private Catholic primary and elementary school owned and run by priests, with a mission to educate young boys and prepare them for secondary levels. It was quite big with many trees that were home to local birds. The playgrounds included a real size Football field, as well as many other fields for Basketball, Volleyball fields and other kind of sports. Each grade had five or six classes, formed of 30 to 40 students. The responsibilities were divided between two supervisors, while the priests only gave us Catechism, positive vibes and some smiles. To keep control of the big number of kids, each grade was allowed to use and play in certain zones.

The school was surrounded by high fences, a few gates, a stadium-style concrete seating, buildings for management… classrooms and of course a church.

In fact, I believe the architect who designed that school didn't bother being creative or innovative. The corridors, the classes and the washrooms were plain and simple. However, it was meant to be a nice representation of the peaceful environment we were living in: simple, practical, with a pinch of minimalism, far from any form of luxury and amidst lots of greenery.

After the war started, the school couldn't keep up with the rapid pace or war and didn't change anything; its walls were heavily marked with bullet holes and other signs of violence.

In fact, they managed to maintain the interior so well, but unfortunately, they found it useless to cover any of the bullet holes showing on the outside walls.

Maybe they meant to make the kids feel safer once they were inside the school, as if all the war madness was over. My primary years, we were only allowed to play in a big plain playground, and of course, we used to play pretend. Some of us were the police, others the criminals, the good guys versus the bad guys or right versus wrong we thought, unaware of the irony to come.

Outside the walls of the school, we would see the big guys dressed in military uniforms with guns in their hands, looking like "real bad asses".

We were told that they were the good guys, because they were from our tribe protecting us from the villains.

It was the generation influenced by comic books and big encyclopaedias, way before cable TV invaded the young brains and the internet gave them many strange images of heroes, villains, demons and saviours.

I wonder how I used to imagine the bad guys back then.

Were they more like monsters, ugly beasts, rabid animals, or just different-looking humans?

I hardly recall from my earlier years anything other than running down to the shelters and staying there for hours and sometimes even days.

Whoever thought that candlelight was romantic is either delusional or heavily infected with multiple psychological love disorders.

However, those dim lights and their smell of wax were still more luxurious and spirit lifting than sitting in the dark listening to the sound of bombs, as if they were unwanted fireworks. Meanwhile, housewives, older kids, teenagers and non-military grown-up men would spend lots of hours playing cards and other board games…I sometimes wonder if I spent more times in the building's shelter than my own classroom. Where did I learn more? Was it that moment teaching me about the future which now is the past? Or was it the past defining my future? The different time theories in all the diversity and contradictions made little sense to me, it was like trying to prove the Big Bang, or predict the Big Crunch or the Big Freeze.

How big a question can be and how important is it to a mouse running on a wheel? Big hearts, big brains, big muscles, big problems, big lies, big trucks, Big Ben, BIG, BIG, BIG! Why are we so obsessed with big things?

These questions keep stirring within me, drawing my perception of existence to a higher perspective.

A possibility that I'm the unlucky one living this miserable reality while at least one version of me is having better luck living in a parallel universe with no hate and no war, or even better, a universe of infinite pleasures: candies, booze, chocolate, ecstasy or whatever material makes a person happy.

Would that even be possible?

I had never considered those options at that time. Even though I was regularly visited by Peter Pan, Baby Jesus and some of his angels…none of them had any interest in enlightening me. They just popped up, kept me company and shared my war experiences.

Sometimes they were ironically funny, and other times, they were helpful, helping me create a different reality, an imaginary better life.

As the gods of yesterday became the myths of today, the gods of today will become the myths of tomorrow. Relatively everything is possible and there could be an infinite amount of realities.

Going back to the same year Miss Evil slapped me, a light wind of change blew through my soul. I felt, behaved and acted as a reborn new kid. I seemed fearlessly confident, and then I started bullying other kids, choosing to be the criminal on the playground.

To be honest, there were no apparent psychological consequence to a particular pat event. It was a wake-up call, with all the war and bad shit surrounding my daily routine, I suddenly decided not be the good guy anymore, and in a way, it worked to my advantage.

The days passed quickly until one day, our school's daily routine was interrupted and we were all sent home earlier. We used to celebrate a day like this, where a fight started somewhere, schools shut down their doors, deciding not to take any risks and giving security a priority over education.

However, that day I was in the playground tripping other kids and putting them in jail…oh yes, I was the bad cop, I was respected and feared at the same time, even by older kids. The bell rang, interrupting my glorious police operation. The teachers took us to our classes while whispering rumors/ real time events, then parents came to pick us up and take us home.

There was anger, fear and long faces that I couldn't understand.

It was only when we reached my neighbourhood that I started to figure out the gravity of the situation.

The silence was interrupted by women crying and screaming in the distance.

The smell of burning wheels mixed with blood was making its way through my nose and settling in my throat.

It was a taste of cowardice, weakness, horror and death.

An uncontrollable invasion of goosebumps, accompanied with the feeling of impotence and disbelief.

The sight of the deserted streets was truly reflecting an evacuated warzone.

On the way back home, I was told that a large bomb had hit a restaurant across our building, no more and no less, end of conversation.

There was no need for any words, I saw the destruction, few burning cars and a lot of blood on the asphalt.

At the entrance of our building, in the same place my cousin left his backpack not long ago, were bloodstains.

Surprisingly, it wasn't something I reacted strongly to. It looked like extra ketchup on a cheap burger.

Later that day, I found out that it was the blood of an 18-year-old guy, a cool pacifist neighbour that refused to join any militia or get involved in the war. Instead, he chose to go to university, and in his free time, he used to take care of me, got me little toys, took me for walks and gave me some motivational talks to relieve me of the war traumas.

I don't remember his name or how he looked like, but I will never forget how nice he was to me and the fact that he had a hidden crush on my older sister 'Venus'.

To this day, that school day cut short off is one of my worst memories. After the fire was put out, a body count started:

1. The nice guy and his best friend, both so young and in their first year of university.
2. Our pacifist neighbour and his best friend, both hard working with no interest in joining a militia or carrying a weapon.
3. The sister of my mom's best friend. She was young, engaged and about to get married. I'm sure she would have made a beautiful bride.
4. Another young guy that I used to salute on a daily basis. He would play with me at times.

He had recently joined a militia to defend us from the villains, but he still had that innocent smile, so I guess he hadn't killed or seen anyone killing before he passed away.

Those were the ones I knew and talked to on a daily basis. The civilian death toll was much higher and it took years for the tears of the survivors and their relatives to dry.

Not all war games were that dramatic though, some had a better ending like for example, the two young twin sisters who were walking back from school, holding each other's hands, planning the rest of their play day, and unaware that the future would hold unpleasant surprises.

A small rocket hit a building nearby causing damages but no casualties. Both girls were terrified, their reaction was to run, but as one of the girls looked at the other, she started screaming. Her beloved other half was covered with blood from her face all the way down…The bloody girl looked at her sister in turn and froze in her place, staring at her sister with fear and agony. While one was screaming from fear, the other was traumatised as if she saw a ghost.

Apparently, she was looking at the little neck of her sister. It was spraying blood all over. In fact, it was a strange ricochet, a tiny piece of the projectile had bounced far away and penetrated the little body hitting a vein.

Two eight-years-old girls were standing there traumatised, but one of them got a blood bath while the other got carried by a stranger with just a towel to stop the bleeding. She made it to a hospital and an operation saved her life but left a huge scar and a terrifying first war memory.

So many other stories of holy interventions that made someone miss an appointment, skip an important meeting or avoid a supposedly safe road…unreasonable decisions and unrealistic actions saved many lives.

Cheating death was becoming more and more common, many kids and adults had so traumatic stories, that were surely marked and, in their memories, but sometimes on their bodies as well.

It wasn't like playing chess with death. A chess player needs: problem-solving skills, abstract reasoning, patience calmness and other qualities and skills…it was neither playing poker nor street dice…However, it was all a game, a war game. Some people died while others survived.

Life Goes On

One thing these events taught me very well was that life goes on…that is, if the bombs didn't kill you.

I mean, they were just like a routinely dusting job, get it done as fast as possible, and once the task is accomplished, they become an old memory. Most fade quickly like the names and characters I forgot or some random passing events that were less relevant to me.

On one hand it was too bad for those who died. On the other hand, the ones who survived had some consolation because the souls of their deceased were freed from this hard life.

They were gone to a better place, a place called Heaven, where there are angels, a moderate weather, other nice people and most importantly, no war…They called it paradise, but could it be a parallel universe or maybe a different dimension?

These consolations were no more different than our first Persian cat 'Pousy' got lost. She got out of my dad's car window that was slightly opened tiny opened and never came back. We looked everywhere but there was no trace of her. By the end of the day, my sister and I were crying while the grown-ups were telling us: "Don't worry, she'll be fine… someone will find her…she will be in a better place."

We shed so many tears that our parents bought us a new kitten. She was almost identical. We even gave her the same name.

All lives come to an end, whichever it is a tree, a pet, a wild animal, a human, a planet, a star… Nowadays, intellectuals have developed many theories about life after death, but nothing was more creative than or as interesting as the concept of paradise, hell, reincarnation, or any other older myths and religions.

Whether the new theories are better than the old ones, whether our life matters at all, or whether we exist or not…the question remains the same: What's the purpose of life?

It must have been that bomb that transformed me from being a bully to becoming a daydreamer or what I like to call 'a seeker of a higher truth'.

My grades suddenly started dropping and my school days were becoming a staring competition.

I used to sit and stare at the teacher, the board or anything that grabbed my attention.

It took my teachers a while to notice my lack of focus, but fortunately I was still in a safe zone and passed my exams even though the grades were failing rapidly.

On the playground, I was no longer interested in games. The other kids felt the changes much faster than the grown-ups. Probably because the teachers were too busy reciting the lessons to themselves, listening to the echo of their own words. Forgetting the teacher's role in observing the kids.

Not that I blame them, in the end, they were living the same war. They were terrified from certain kids, because one of their dads could be a militia man, a serial killer or a psychopath…I could see on their faces fear and weakness.

The battle of doing the right thing continued playing in front of my eyes, and I learned that the needs justify the means…Nothing is wrong and nothing is right, it's just another theory waiting to be debunked.

But this was such a bad period that parents had no time to listen to their children, a perfect atmosphere for a paedophilic teacher to take advantage of some unfortunate young boys. Everyone was busy with surviving, and somehow the stars aligned for the bad guys to take advantage of the circumstances.

It only took the other kids a few days to stop picking me in their teams. I was left to daydream on my own. I still never got bullied, probably because they must have been scared of waking the beast in me again. Everybody left me alone, even at home my parents were a little busy. The people who died in that bomb could never be replaced, like 'Pousy'.

Getting Numb

The most important point in history is with no doubt 'the present', which realistically isn't much different from the past. Two or three years went by and nothing changed, for me at least.

Politicians and militias were changing alliances; Yesterday's enemies were becoming today's allies, and then again, back to changing sides, falling into a never-ending vicious circle…

No one could understand that mess.

It was easier to comprehend the concept of quantum theory and entangled particle…Mathematics supported by some philosophy and physics is supposed to give a certain explanation to make these theories approachable within the realm of human comprehension…Understanding what the hell was going on in the years that followed had no logic. It's like trying to solve pi, no matter how smart, persistent and dedicated a scientist is, the damn number will keep on going forever.

The world was dealing with this kind of equation, but for us children, we only knew that we were still at war.

More bombs, explosions and assassinations were happening weekly and sometimes daily. It was so constant that it stopped being irrational.

Just as car explosions in my neighbourhood stopped being 'news', there were fewer casualties and less concerns. Nothing was happening, or in maybe nothing felt significant and relatable to me.

In a way, I developed a denial reaction about reality, I was living on the margin, waiting to hear about some new people who travelled to the place called Heaven.

Everything seemed normal for a while and I strongly believed that nothing could shock me.

I was still riding my bike on the streets, daring those snipers at times and gambling with my life…Some days, I would play Football with my friends between the ruins and other days our playground would be a parking lot with unexploded bombs, we would live totally unaware of the danger we were facing.

Our favourite pass time was collecting, exchanging and playing with marbles. We used to treasure them as if they were precious stones, planets, moons and stars.

Our daily routine was usually always interrupted by bombs or snipers…A little bit of fear and some tears, then life used to go on as if nothing happened.

Could human natures be that unessential? Could letting go be a blessing?

Could a society be considered as one or a whole?

Individuals are vulnerable to many disorders and diseases such as Alzheimer's, in which the brain's cells die progressively and at variable rates…

Unlike the myth of beer and liquors that kill the brain's cells at night and the orange juice that helps to regenerate new ones in the morning, the symptoms of Alzheimer's disease worsen over time with little to no chance of improvement; Facts, ideas, dreams and memories get all mixed up and things only get worse.

My fellow countrymen suffered from the same symptoms, it was almost like a mass hallucination that made them fight, pray and weep.

From the long existence of our ancestors on earth, we only remember a little.

We forgot our origins, our creators, we lost some high advanced technologies and we mixed reality with myths… Nobody gave a shit about those anomalies, kids waited for the ceasefire times to go on the streets and be kids. I had my pockets full of marbles labelled as "normal ones, old ones and special ones" … always searching for a weak opponent to take advantage of…

We took those games seriously and collected those marbles as if they were diamonds. A bomb once fell nearby and created a chaos between the five young players. Three kids ran away with fear leaving everything behind them, while me and another kid started collecting the pieces as fast as we could, giving those cheap items more value than our own safety. To me, a single marble was as significant as the two-billion-year-old sphere found in South Africa. Why would I care about the past since I'm not sure about the present? Why would any human care?

Our species suffer from dementia, Atlantis never existed. There are no lost civilisations that left their million-year-old footprints, and definitely no time travellers with a dark sense of humour who left clues behind them, such as a three-hundred-million-year-old screw and a four-hundred-million-year-old hammer… It's so funny how such a measly discovery can dazzle the biggest and brightest minds and keep us in the dark, afraid of rewriting our history.

I just wonder if these tools were kept underground for us to find, or if it was it a prop mistake like the ones you see in some of the most successful high budget movies.

Was it a nasty trick played on us, in the time of high tech? The truth is that we still can't figure out the technologies used thousands of years ago.

What if our far ancestors knew some secrets unknown to us? Did they know more about immortality or life after death?

To be honest, at that age I didn't care much about those questions. My main goal was reaching puberty…Becoming a man.

I was chasing that dream, the illusion of becoming an adult, fighting the bad guys, protecting the innocents, having a fast sports car, a gun and of course some attractive girls. Only a couple of years passed since my first slap, so much and nothing had happened… But to my surprise, my first step to manhood finally came, I got my first gun!

It was a 6 mm automatic gun, small enough to fit in a young boy's hand, loud enough to make it sound serious and efficient enough to wound someone from a long range or kill from a shorter range…

At first, I started shooting at cans, bottles and still targets, with some responsible supervision, but then to my surprise, the gun was forgotten with me as if it was a harmless toy. Like any ambitious kid would do, I started practising on living targets, mostly lizards, mice and rats.

My behaviour wasn't much different from the scientist experimenting on animal labs. Domesticating other species is a characteristic of human's evolution and as a kid I was taking the right path.

Owning a gun had far more psychological effects than one would imagine.

It gave me a sense of superiority, not over friends and other human beings but over other species. Superiority over creatures that were defenceless against such brutal and evil power.

In fact, even though physicists, mathematicians, and philosophers came up with theories, machines and inventions that shaped our history… It was only because of men with guns that we conquered the planet and shaped it the way it looks today.

Being that young and owning a gun wasn't something unusual. That's how kids were prepared 'physically and emotionally' to be part in the war.

Summertime was the training season. Leaving the city and going to the mountains, that was the good life.

There was a big compound in the middle of a peaceful village, with wild berries, vineyards, apple and peach trees… There was even a pine forest with a big camping area which made it a perfect retirement spot. It looked so serene, far away from war. That's exactly where the militia training camp was set up.

I had my mountain bike, my gun, many friends, my dog Lucky and lots of freedom. All these elements gave me the feeling of becoming a man. I must admit, I was getting really good at shooting that I could pass for one of those characters in an old western movie.

But the summer didn't last long, and as soon as school started again, I was back to my useless books instead of the mighty gun.

The illusion of becoming a man would end each September, and then the negative vibes would start again and get accentuated.

Venus

During winter time, many animals hibernate, as did my gun…

I was back to being a school child…while my dad was still away somewhere on a certain frontier fighting the bad guys, fornicating or shooting at cans.

My lack of fatherly affection was replaced easily. I was lucky because at night, I could choose between sleeping next to my mom or next to my loving oldest sister.

I had two eldest sisters, leaving me to be the spoiled little one. While the middle sister was more of a friend of mine, a companion and a partner in crime, my eldest belonged to a different age group.

She was 16 years old at the time, full of youth and gifted with raw beauty. For schoolmates, neighbours and total strangers, she was like a celebrity or a beauty queen, but for me, she was the sweetest person on earth.

I always sensed a mysterious hidden melancholia when I used to be around her…But maybe, I was too young for her to share with me any of her fears, dreams or passions.

I only knew that older guys were nice to me and always asked me questions about her…simple things like: 'How is your sister?', 'What is she doing these days?', 'Is she too busy with school?', 'Any plans for the weekend?'

My answers were always short and innocent: 'yes', 'no' and 'I don't know'.

Most of these tricky conversations that interrupted my play time would end with a request such as: 'Send her my regards'.

I never forgot to deliver their messages and she always answered me with a smile no more and no less.

It would only be fair to say that she was my Venus; more like a planet, a goddess or an angel.

While everybody was busy fighting, hating and grieving… My Venus used to brighten my darkest moments and take care of me, she woke me up every morning, either with a kiss or by dressing me up in bed and getting me ready to go to school. After school, she used to help me with my homework and my daily growing up routines. Anytime I needed her, she was always there for me…And I loved that.

Nothing last forever same as nothing can travel through a blackhole in the universe, not even the light can escape from its gravitational grasp… It's still a mysterious and strange phenomenon that fascinates astronomers and curious minds.

However, this event was not strange to me, blackholes have been surrounding me ever since I could remember…The rays of light never lasted too long and they vanished so fast that I thought I was the one attracting all this matter to my sad reality.

Self-blaming is very common with traumatised people and especially kids; It leads to the feeling of guilt, agony, depression and other serious psychological problems.

I remember that specific early morning as if it was yesterday. My sister woke me up and helped me get ready to school; she gave me my daily dose of love, a big hug, a kiss and lots of positive energy.

She was still feeling proud of an incident that happened two days earlier.

She was returning back home with the school bus as usual, when a loud explosion followed by broken glass happened a few metres away. The bus was forced to stop because it was about to catch fire and the kids would have gotten burned alive…

While most children panicked, my sister acted like a responsible mature and caring adult. My version of Wonder Woman! She calmed the younger kids, forced some orders, then stopped the crying and the chaos.

It was such an act of bravery that the bus driver informed the school director. Next day, she was praised by everybody and my parents received a recognition letter for her positive attitude.

I still remember the amount of pride that reflected on her face, but that ray of light didn't last too long, because that early morning I felt like I shouldn't go to school, and I didn't want to leave her side.

It took her 15 minutes or more to wake me up. Dressing me was an even harder task…I cried and said to my mom:

"I'm not feeling well, please let's not leave the house."

Of course, my mom did the right thing, she checked my temperature, asked me for the reason I didn't want to go… then told me to get ready and to stop acting like a spoiled baby.

A superstitious person would have said something like:

It was the constellations' positioning, the planets' line up, the God's mood or the humans' impact on Mother Nature's selection of the fittest.

I just remember having an awkward feeling, I didn't want to leave bed; I wanted that hug to last all day in order not to get out of the house.

It was an unusual behaviour from my side, since I never complained about going to school…

Some might call it a sixth sense, a warning from my guardian angel or a message from the future…Whatever it was I just felt the waves of a disaster coming from beyond where my vision could reach…My animal instinct could feel that tsunami hitting my shore of safety.

A half day at school, full of malaise for no apparent reason…I rushed back home to find out that my Venus had collapsed.

A mysterious unexplained accident. While talking to her friends, she just fell. She didn't hit her head or hurt herself in any way. She just laid there on the floor till she was taken to the hospital, where she just settled on a bed in a deep sleep, a coma.

Coma

Some say that the planet Venus was once alive, with waterfalls, rivers and oases, and with a day as long as 225 earth days!

What a life it would be, had I been born on planet Venus in its 'Belle Époque'.

I can imagine being born in the morning and waiting 225 days to see my first sunset…Time would be passing so slow and life would be so easy.

But something really bad must have happened for Venus to turn into a hell, slowly die or maybe go into a silent long-lasting coma. Its harsh volcanic nature made spacecrafts melt like ice cream on a hot summer's day, then we humans sent three probes then decided to continue watching that bright planet from afar.

The universe is a mystery; its components are full of stories hidden all over. And we humans are curious creatures that have always been fascinated by the skies. That's why we started writing stories of all sorts like diaries, myths, fiction and many more genres… The oldest surviving manuscripts were neither e-books nor paper, they were stories inscribed on stone.

We know very little about our past! Maybe because our ancestors only started writing their stories, inventions and discoveries on paper or saving it on hard drives and clouds. No wonder we were in a coma all these years.

Suddenly, we wake up and find mega structures all over our planet with no indication or clue on how they were built.

Structures that we are unable to replicate in our current timeline, even though we sent a man to the moon, built a space station and we landed probes on Mercury, Venus, Mars, Jupiter and Saturn…We've come a long way from the Stone Age but we still can't figure out how it was built.

As soon as we opened our eyes, everything around us had changed. Atlantis no longer existed, the Mayans abandoned their cities, and the gods in our history were becoming legends and mythical figures.

I was living one of those complex stories, a chaotic mess with dramatic characters, unrealistic plots and illogical subplots and strings that were tangled with different timelines, realities or fictions.

I came back from school to see my mom in tears of despair, holding on to any glimpse of hope. I was told that Venus fell and went to the hospital just to recover and come back to us. I couldn't believe that these tears the cause were just a small accident; And so I instinctively turned to God praying and promising him future good deeds in exchange for her recovery.

When medicine seems to have no answer, we remember our faith, start praying and begging for a divine intervention.

A story was being written with pain and tears, but would that story survive? Do stories have a lifespan just as anything else?

Our most recognised stories are a few thousand years old.

The lost paradise, the great flood, the tower of Babel and the apocalypse…these ancient stories cover a wide range of genres such as, history, adventure, biography, action, myths and sci-fi.

They give us a very small/ a glimpse of the age of our planet and less than a noticeable fraction in the life span of the universe.

All those books that survived, 'old and recent', are nothing in comparison to Mother Nature's great stories. They were written throughout the years on most of our planet's stones, our mountains, the moon and every planet we can think of.

Is the universe playing a trick on us?

Did all the planets in our solar system go into a coma? Is it a form of hibernation?

Some great minds and futuristic visionaries insist that humanity's only hope of survival is to colonize other planets. The more pretentious solution goes as far as talking about the need to colonize other galaxies.

Unfortunately, our life span is too short for these types of travels.

Aging reversal is an option, humans of course could get to lengthen their life by reversing the process of ageing.

If an elite group achieves that scientifically possible process, people would be able to live up to hundred or thousand years.

The irony is that we still wouldn't be doing anything special, we would just be copying nature's way (nature's process, the natural process of life…).

Turtles, crocodiles and bowhead whales keep on growing and never age. Some of these creatures can do unimaginable things like repairing damaged DNA or living without oxygen…Their bodies do not sag; they never get wrinkled or weak until they die.

Lobsters and some jellyfish are even called biologically immortal… They must be killed by diseases or other predators, otherwise they will live forever.

Forget about the elixir of life that baffled wizards, alchemists and kings of the past. Ageing reversal is humanity's next big thing, even though it might have different themes, the goal remains the same.

The fact is that at our time, human life's expectancy is increasing, due to medicine and healthy modern lifestyles, but it consists of: 40% sleeping, 10% eating, 5% working out, 5% personal hygiene needs and other distractions of our daily life such as taking a leak, pooing, having intercourse, etcetera…

With all that limited time to do things that matter, people still find time to make wars.

In my simple young mind, I thought that my sister was an experimental astronaut; I saw her motionless in the hospital bed a few times and didn't like it. I hated looking at the heartbeat monitor and despised the breathing tube.

I couldn't look into her eyes, they were half open but staring at the void or another dimension that neither me, nor the doctors could have figured out. I convinced myself that she was hibernating and that sooner or later she would snap out of it and say "surprise!"

And that we would all be happy with that nasty prank she was playing on us, we would give her a big hug and say "we love you."

Every action has a higher purpose, and the only hope of survival for our species is to learn how to hibernate, just like bears and other animals but in a more controlled and effective way.

Space travel would require 'hibernation chambers', and the astronauts should be fully aware that they would stop ageing while using them. That's what my sister was doing, testing out that knowledge by going on a space mission. At least, that's what I told myself.

I counted the days as they were passing and my sister was still hibernating…days, weeks and months passed, until I lost track and stopped counting.

It was too hard to keep up with the accumulation of prayers, candles, hopes, dreams and illusions…

Until that night when I heard the sounds of the machines that started beeping gently and gradually ending with panic.

Time to wake up, wake up! Wake up! Destination reached! Wake up!

Hibernation mode ended. Wake up! Terminate, disable, abort…wake up!

Mission failed, she never woke up and my space scenario didn't end as planned.

Maybe she faced an unexpected malfunction, or maybe she decided there's nothing worth fighting for…

I would never know, but that day something hit me so hard, I became numb, senseless, floating in the same space my sister had tried to explore…There were and still are no words that could describe the sensation.

If I was a rock, the tears would have written that specific part of the story, but for a human, a child, it was the start of a new phase with less faith and more carelessness.

There was lots of crying, whining, grieving…and a last goodbye…a funeral.

The Funeral

Funerals are weird ceremonies, like a sad wedding, especially for younger people. Families, relatives and friends are emotionally devastated, and most of the time a hysterical trance state looms over the room where a well-dressed corpse in full make up lies still in the bed.

For older deceased people, it's more like a farewell, families' behaviours are less dramatic. They don't show any sign of relief, but deep inside, everybody knows, it's a heavy load removed from society's shoulders.

In both cases, it's a useless tradition that societies developed over the centuries to share their pain with others...

Why? Because just like wolves, chimpanzees, elephants, ravens, dolphins and many others, we are social species.

Each civilisation or religious group have their own customs, practices and different traditions.

Some get buried in coffins, others under the soil or at sea. Some even burn corpses, or smash their bones into small pieces and leave them on a mountaintop to be decomposed and eaten by vultures.

Newer methods such as: cremation, promession, or biodegradable burial which turns a corpse into a tree or an internal reef...

I imagine future methods will be space burials on selected planets or moons.

Why would humans go through all this for body disposal?

What happened to mummification and preserving the corpse for as long as possible?

I could never understand these rituals, or their purpose which always seemed vague to me…

In my opinion, the idea of keeping a corpse in a cemetery to go visit, pray for, or pay respect to is bizarre. But it is part of our culture and a ritual been practised for as far as I remember.

In fact, as archaeologists tell us, people built gigantic pyramids and mega structures with very primitive tools to let someone rest in peace.

It's a horrendous story, but our societies have always been filled with fools looking for immortality.

I must say, it's not as glorious as watching the death of a star, which is inevitable and the day will come when our sun will run out of its fuel, expand to a red giant star and burn or swallow all the planets going around it. The end is the same for everybody, rich, poor, stupid or wise. Humans and stars will all turn to their initial form: Dust.

Millions of years will pass, and that same stardust will be part of forming new planets and stars. What a vicious tedious circle of life.

So why shed a tear? Why weep for such a show?

I remember the corpse laying on what became later my bed. The denial, the sympathy and the hope of an afterlife, I could see all these beliefs or might I say illusions on people's faces.

I could hear others whispering about the unfairness of life and the cruelty of God.

My great-grandfather was sitting on a chair all alone,

he was in his ninety something and tears dried up… His mission in this war was to walk through snipers and explosions every day for the sole purpose of visiting his grandchildren and offer them candies and small gifts. He always used to carry an extra paper bag full of treats to give to the kids he would meet along the way… He was our real-life Santa Claus.

Even though he was a happy old man with lots of positive energy, I could imagine he was bored of life and was suffering from his ageing body.

I wonder if the snipers that used to see him cross the streets, had agreed not to shoot him, because no one ever tried to, not even the new snipers who needed to practice shooting.

Was it because he was old? Or was he invisible to death?

All the kids were thankful to whatever reason or superpower kept him alive, but that day, I could see him muttering all alone on his chair…

He was in retreat, as if he was living in his own world. I got a little closer and I could hear him arguing with God:

"Why?" he muttered. "Why the poor young child? I'm old enough, why don't you take me instead?"

He kept asking the same question in different forms. "Why, God, why?"

"Don't you have mercy on her, on her parents and loved ones? Do you think it's fair for her? For me? For her parents?"

Being that old is a blessing; he was invisible and inaudible to the rest of the crowd in that room.

Maybe the snipers didn't see him after all; nature has mysterious ways to protect some of us.

A fawn is born odourless. It's Mother Nature's way of giving it protection from predators. Even the mama doe doesn't argue with mama nature and stays away from the fawn for a few days to protect it from its own scent.

My great-grandfather had a real superpower after all, he was a super hero and the war didn't kill him; he died many years later from boredom and loneliness.

Other Superheroes

Wars create superheroes.

During peacetime, the most heroic thing a hero could do is to feed the poor, help an old lady cross the street, or maybe even save a pet stuck on a tree.

There are even honourable and heroic jobs for superheroes in times of peace.

A firefighter, a negotiator, a book consultant or even a taxi driver…Someone with a job like that could save your life and, or money. Unfortunately, the impact of these service jobs is not recognized enough in our society. It seems as if they are taken for granted when in fact, they are essential to improve the quality of our society.

Some wars are fought without weapons and its heroes are Saints; Others are philosophers and poets…Words can be so efficient and crucial, that they could change the course of events and sometimes history.

However, this fight for heroism is comparable to one we used to call as children "a spitting war":

What's a "spitting war"? let me explain:

It's like a verbal war but spits would be replacing words.

It's humiliating, but the worst that could happen is getting wet…Imagine if our war was a similar one: East and West, people on both sides standing, cursing, shouting and screaming at each other, the anger building up then came the first spit. And just like that the war starts, and at the end of it, the winner would be the one with stinker breath and nothing more.

My "époque" was modern though, guns were so abundant and played a big role in creating the villains and the superheroes.

The rise of humanity started with a stone, a simple tool like a stick, an arrow then a sword…Those objects kept on developing slowly and gave us the advantage over all other earth creatures.

In a way, it helped our species to have power, dominance and an advantage on other creatures. It made us think and feel invincible and aided us in developing impressive supernatural abilities.

Heroism came later in history, it stemmed from our natural instinct and the search for food and protection. It then it became a complex psychological disorder, a symptom of God complex.

Was it inherited from our ancestors millions of years ago? Or developed in parallel with the tools?

By the time humans invented wheels, cars and robots, those mental illnesses were increasing so much and developing at a faster pace than rising technologies.

The disorders got worse with modernity, individuals and nations owning weapons that ranged from a little pocket knife to a nuclear bomb and other weapons of massive destruction.

After my sister's death, I changed again…The dreamer searching for answers vanished, and I became 'a distracted cuckoo kid' living on the moon, anywhere that was out of this world.

At first, teachers were sympathetic and let me be.

Other times, our young English teacher would allow me to sit on her desk and stare at her legs every day.

At other times, she would send me to the math teacher, a middle-aged man who had a crush on her.

Like Kent Clark, he had multiple identities, teaching the kids and defending the sexy young teacher by day, and calculating his targets and launching bombs by night. He must have been proud or maybe felt at times superior to Superman because he didn't have to hide his second identity behind a suit and eyeglasses. He just came to school every morning, pretending that it was just another normal day, convincing himself that he's doing the right thing.

But he wasn't the only hero we had; others were less apparent to the naked eye. Most teachers, however, looked sad while others looked like they were on the edge of a break down.

After all, the war was still going on, and people were dying on a daily basis. The teachers lost track, forgot about children's traumas and started treating all kids equally.

Some had a long and thick wooden ruler with a sharp metal on the edge to terrorise the already traumatised kids, others used their words as swords to deepen our suffering.

In a way, each of these teachers were superheroes and they would make us feel it with their sense of entitlement in the classroom, as if they were superior to us and we were privileged to be educated by them.

As time went by, it became hard to differentiate between the harmless, the funny, the abusive and the fake heroes.

Back to my Math teacher, one night he was walking down a dark street in a neighbourhood with no electricity or basic human needs and saw a military vehicle.

Its light was the only source of light, breaking the deadly horror movie-inspired atmosphere.

The vehicle's running engine noise was drowned by loud voices, screaming, shouting and swearing; only interrupted by the sound of a beating and sounds that could either be from an action movie or a beginner drummer practising.

With confident steps, he walked towards the source of that sound and the voices were getting louder; he started to become a little agitated, but instead of stopping, he walked faster till he reached the mystery scene.

There he saw two young men in their mid-twenties, wearing worn-up military uniforms, boots unpolished and covered with dust and scratches…The two militants were obviously having fun. They had a hostage, whose hands were tied in front of him. One of the militants was spitting on the supposedly captured villain, the other militant was laughing loudly and swearing; he had the other end of the rope and was tying it to the vehicle.

He saw all this in a flash of a second and ran to stop the savagery. He went to the first guy, slapped him with his right hand, and then with no hesitation, he slapped the second guy…

The militants were shocked, even the hostage was speechless and stopped moaning and screaming for a while.

"What are you doing? Who are you?" exclaimed one of the militants.

He simply answered, "I'm a teacher."

"Then get the hell out of here before you get hurt…this scumbag is a sniper that killed so many of our friends and families."

The second militant continued, "We are going to teach him a lesson and show him and his brothers how they'll end up for shooting at us."

"We'll drag him behind our jeep around the neighbourhood, and after his skin peels off on the asphalt and he slowly dies, we'll dump his body close to the frontiers."

The teacher was still quiet and both men laughed while the captured sniper started crying and begging for mercy.

"Please let me go, I have children please, please." Then he looked at the teacher. "Mercy…might your merciful God save me…Please."

At that moment, the teacher faced the two young militants and courageously spoke out.

"Shame on you! All of you! Where is your humanity?"

He looked at the tortured man and shouted, "You are an animal, shooting kids and people that have nothing to do with the war!"

Then turned to face the militants and howled: "This man might be fighting on the other side, but he's your brother in humanity."

"Liberty, equality, and fraternity are the soul of our humanity, and without them, we are just animals."

Then he kept on preaching them about the morals, the virtues and the holiness of our souls.

The two militants realised what monsters they were becoming and started crying. They apologised to the teacher and asked forgiveness from God. Then they said that they will take the captured man to the army and let him get a fair civile trial.

You might think that I was dreaming or reading a screenplay from Superdupont, the Franco-Belgian version of Superman.

But in fact, it was a story narrated to us by our science teacher, who happened to be French.

Why would someone tell such a story to kids?

Weren't kids traumatised enough from the daily war events?

And why the fuck would a French teacher live in such a war zone?

It was the same teacher who bullied me for 'daydreaming' during one of his classes. Actually, my friend and I had both forgotten the science book and we were sitting on the first row of the class pretending to look innocent.

That didn't help much; he called with that same tone of his story, "What are you doing? Where's your book?"

We both stayed speechless mumbling, looking at each other as if to say, "It's not me, it's him."

He called my friend first, and as he got closer to him, he grabbed him by the cheeks and started pulling and pinching.

While my friend was crying and begging for mercy, I was waiting for my turn. It didn't take long before he grabbed my cheeks in the same torturous style.

Cheeks pinching! It sounds like a harmless punishment, but when my cheeks were stretched like rubber elastics, I really wished I was that militant from his story, with a rifle in my hand.

Maybe, that hero's mission was recruiting future heartless militants after all…

For months, I had plans for that teacher. I kept on running the same scenario in my head: I'll wait in an alley, he shows up with his clumsy look and walk, I'll stand in front of him and say *"Salut, Monsieur."* I'll smile as he nods his head politely, then without saying another word, I'll point my gun at him.

He'll start saying things in French, then he'll turns away to run. Finally, I'll shoot him in his butt, get him on his knees and teach him a lesson about violence and bullying young kids; *Voila, Monsieur!*

Fortunately, I didn't have to do any of this, because a year later, revenge came unexpectedly…Our French Superhero was facing karma.

Karma

Hinduism is considered to be one of the oldest surviving religions; it has stories of flying gods coming from the skies, nuclear explosions, galactic wars and the famous story of the great flood.

That particular story has been repeated by almost every ancient culture and religion. A few versions just mention a flood with some sort of storyline; however, many versions consist of the same plot. Names and characters might have changed from a book to another, but the similarity makes it shockingly evident.

Not to mention, the most recent version that tells a different story about a storage of animal's DNA instead of the physical animals on one boat...which is like the disclaimer we read at the end of the movies: "no animals were harmed" means less worry about the animals and the captain.

Science has been searching for evidence of such an event and most geologists agree that at the end of the ice age, a flood or many floods happened after the glacial period, they estimate it to be somewhere around 15,000 years ago.

Anyhow, Hinduism is a very interesting religion historically, socially and anthropologically. In addition to all those myths and beliefs, it introduces the concept of karma, which survived several years of changes to finally become a universal concept that surpasses the original.

It has nothing to do with the faith of reincarnation and Hinduism anymore. Many pious people, regardless of religion, believe in that simplified theory: Karma is a force of God, Mother Nature or aliens, for all we know, which means that what goes around comes around. Every person committing an act of kindness initiates a wave of positive vibes which results in positive things coming back to them, similarly, any act of evil.

For every action, there's a reaction, and life never rewards those who don't deserve it.

Mr Superdupont was still teaching using his classic way, preaching at times and using violence on others.

Until one day during the break, Mr Superdupont noticed some foolish behaviour that could not be ignored and hit one of my classmates with a wooden ruler on his arm.

That young boy was a couple of years older than me and the rest of my classmates. To describe the victim fairly, I must mention that he was not a very smart boy but he was good hearted, courageous and always stood up against the bullies.

He had just hit puberty and it showed. He looked like a young man, with toned muscles and a height that qualifies him enough to be a basket-ball player.

We knew that his dad was never home, and rumours were that he was staying in one of the most dangerous war zones. His dad was a legend, even the physics teacher heard about him, but we never saw him at school or anywhere else for a fact. I was sure that my classmate didn't spend too much time with his dad and he never even mentioned him unless it was to seek protection. Those kinds of stories were very common but always hushed or low profile. It was characters that you knew and sometimes saw but couldn't tell if they were real, exaggerated or mythical.

I, personally, never had any problem with him; we were not friends but we also never crossed each other's paths, and not to forget that he was loud which makes me think that he fitted the gangster type. Everybody knew about his recent trauma. An RPJ or another kind of rocket was targeted their house, and as a result the living room was totally destroyed. In addition, fire ravaged the rest of the rooms. He was sleeping in his bedroom and woke up to the fire that started to feed on his skin. He never told anyone the full story, but he came back to school after a long absence with severe three-degree burn wounds on his hands, arms and other parts of his body. He had to cover them with long sleeves to protect his skin from any irritations. We all made sure not to touch him in any way avoid causing him pain.

Mr Superdupont, however, must have been too busy fighting villains at night, he forgot about the kid's special case and that wooden ruler must have caused great pain to the poor boy.

Our young friend cried and screamed at first, crawled down on the floor in agony and pain shouting loudly.

"Ahhhhh, it hurts, it burns, fuuuuck…"

Mr Superdupont was still standing and looking at him with no regrets, as if to say: "You know you deserve this."

Suddenly and as if the pain had just vanished, our friend stood up, his eyes wide and almost rabid, looked Mr Superdupont in the eyes and kicked him in the stomach.

Every kid froze in disbelief, waiting for the superhero's reaction. To our surprise, he started running away and the young boy followed him, reaching him with a few other kicks on the ass while all the other kids were cheering. I was getting ready to trip him up as he was passing next to me, but even that wasn't needed because the young monster jumped on his back and started punching him.

I don't know how long that beating went on for before other teachers interfered, but that was karma. The universe does take care of everything.

To me, that incident was a clear indicator that the relationship and the hierarchy between kids and grown-ups was broken. Fear and violence were becoming the new norm.

A New Era

There was the usual endless war events, the snipers were still terrifying and killing civilians, but as if it wasn't enough, new techniques were added.

TNT explosions were introduced to the equation, packages, cars and trucks started exploding in crowded streets, close to supermarkets, cinemas and other busy locations.

No one ever knew who, where or why those nasty surprises were left in my neighbourhood… And the result was fear amongst us, taking sides and death.

I was still a kid and I had already survived many fatal accidents, the closest was a car explosion across my grandparents' house.

Just after school, I went to have lunch at my grandma's, and instead of having a meal, I got a horror scene, a car exploded leaving few people dead and many injured. The loud bang wasn't what scared me the most, maybe our ears were used to those bangs. My quick reaction might have saved me from flying burning car metal pieces, but it didn't save my eyes from seeing blood and flying body parts…few seconds after the explosions, there was the silence, then the screams and moans of pain. I turned around to run back home and on the floor right in front of me was a decapitated leg.

I prayed to God, might the Almighty hit the rewind button and stop this horror from happening, and I ran as fast as I could but nothing could erase those images from my head. Later that day, I realised that the leg was that of my friend's mother.

She survived; she had grocery bags in her hands when the explosion happened; her kids and husband were waiting for her at home so they could have the family lunch. Unfortunately, that day she didn't make it back at time.

The TNT kept on popping here and there for different reasons and different targets.

It might have been a practice period because later on, those TNT were used to assassinate leaders. I even suspected that some of them were placed in areas just to cause fear. Nothing made sense and all we could do was pray for the end of this horror show.

The trend was switching from classic militia confrontations to internal conflicts and coups.

Some called it house cleanliness, internal reorganising or a restructuring.

Civilians lived the same scenario over and over again; a party or a militia would take different side get, then fight each other like a two-headed viper fighting itself over dinner.

The direct consequences were dividing the allies. I saw my uncles, my dad and some old neighbours who carried their weapons at the start of the war for the same reason and fought on the same side, fighting against each other, fleeing to other zone areas, getting captured, jailed or massacred. The end result was always the same.

More war casualties, more money and weapons provided, new leaders emerging, new weaker militias, ~~and~~ smaller parties followed with new promises and hopes. In a way, it was one way to keep order and balance amongst the chaos.

The chaos and the repetition of those same coups in all parties from all sides made it clear to any outside observer that it wasn't random. It was a strategy to provide some sort of unity, the potential of having a single party.

More and more divisions were causing brothers, cousins and friends fighting on the same side to wake up one day and find out that their weapons were pointed at each other.

The good thing is that this kind of fight never lasted too long. The losers would flee and the winners would claim the victory of righteousness.

On a personal level, I had the first signs of a certain traumatic disorder. Like all other kids living the same events, either in my neighbourhood or on the opposite side of the war, I never saw an expert or sought help; I believe the psychological and mental issues were still unknown for most people. I believe that at the times, those issues might have been considered less tragic than gastronomic unease or allergies. In a way, all kids in my class had at least some symptoms, but none were diagnosed by our teachers or parents.

While some kids showed signs of violence, others lost interest in learning and in life in general. Personally, I lost respect for the hierarchy and my clashes with the teachers got worse, especially when I started mocking them to their faces.

However, while I was getting punished for not caring, only one teacher accepted my sarcastic approach to life and what's happening around us.

Unlike the rest of the clan, he could understand that I was spacing out because I was on a mission. He called me over once.

Teacher: What's wrong, young man?

Me: Nothing…

Teacher: I know school can be boring at times, but look around you, what do you see?

Me: I see words, letters next to each other, but I don't understand.

Teacher: You will have enough time to find your voice and make up your own language.

After a silent pause and no reaction from me, he continued.

Teacher: Come back to earth, it's not the right time to stay away…you can't escape war this way…this will end anytime soon.

Although I could understand what he was saying, I didn't have an answer. I couldn't even react with a nod; so he took a breath and softly said, "Come back to earth."

I couldn't tell if he meant that I should leave that depression, irritability, aggressive behaviour and mostly carelessness, or that he meant that I should leave my mission on the moon and head back home.

Ironically, my mission on the moon lasted exactly as long as the poor moon manned missions that endured only three years.

According to Nasa, the year 1972 was marked the year of the last man stepping on the moon, and since then no one have tried to land there again.

The Russians, Europeans, Chinese and all other nations just gave up on the race with the Americans. Even though the technology had advanced greatly, no one seemed to have any interest in going again.

Conspiracy theorists talk about fake moon landings, they present all these logical theories and facts, but no one could argue about my stay on the moon, my solitude, my search for truth and the purpose of life.

Just like the Apollo mission didn't come with any answers, and the officials decided that it's too early for a new adventure, or even perhaps there was not much to be discovered; I decided to let go the entire complicated universe and live my childhood the best I could.

I had no idea if I miraculously auto healed; it was a temporary halt till another mission would be launched again. Same as 50 years later, a sudden interest was starting again into returning to the moon.

Getting back to earth after living in space has some side effects for a human body and its brain.

Strangely, humans are the only species on earth that has no skills at birth. New-born babies' existence relies solely on their parents for the first two months of their life. They can't even lift their heads without help, it takes them over a year to make their first steps, and they stay fully dependent on their caretakers for over a decade.

At first sight, any alien visiting our planet would think that those humans don't belong to earth, the process of giving birth to adulthood and the gravity effect on human's bodies defies any logic. Maybe human beings are the aliens on earth.

Since we have been around for thousands of years, adaptation took its course. It's very difficult for us to leave our current habitat and venture into space. There's a price to pay for each adventure we take and living in low or zero gravity would damage our body; it could cause a degradation of the visual acuity, muscle loss and inevitable psychological stress amongst many other problems.

How do we detect these side effects?

The international space station was launched in 1998; a joint project between the USA, Russia, Japan, The European Union and Canada.

Its first long-term residents came back in November 2000. That's how we can be sure that those effects are real and not just theoretical.

That confirms in a way my theory; I had all the symptoms of space travel: my vision started deteriorating, it went from '20/20 visual acuity' to heavily depending on medical sight correction. I felt physically weak, emotionally tired, intellectually slow and I was struggling to fit...

I was struggling to fit in and gain my place in society. Unfortunately, the grown-ups were too busy with their daily war survival worries, the body count, and their hope that all this madness will be over soon.
So, in order to gain back my respect in the pack, I had to show enthusiasm and courage.

On one sunny Sunday in the autumn, I remember that all parties agreed on a ceasefire, my sister and I, impatient and pushed by an unknown force, interrupted a short family visit to head back home.

Mom: If you don't want to stay, go home now.

Me: Yes, I want to go, I have some homework.

Sister: I'll go with him.

Mom: I'll follow you in 15 minutes.

We left and walked away with no bad intentions, but we got distracted. I found myself with my sister and some older kids on the first floor, on a balcony with no fences.

Making clay sculptures and letting them dry on the edge of the balcony. It sounded harmless; it was the first floor after all. But it must have been my vague vision, my weak unstable muscles and a poor judgment that contributed to what happened next.

I find myself speechless with very few words to describe that day. To be honest, I have zero memory of anything happening during, before or after the free fall. It's just a bunch of stories collected throughout the years from witnesses to help me figure out what happened that day. However, none of any big life's events have ever been recorded and documented properly.

Starting from the Big Bang, the mass extinctions, the big flood, the rise and destructions of old civilisations, the dark ages, the American Revolution, World War I and II, the fall of the wall of Berlin, the rise and fall of communism, 9/11 and the war on terrorism…all the way to our present society's bubbly events.

Even with all the spywares and lack of privacy, major occurrences are surrounded with secrecy and mysteries.

Nothing is as simple as it looks. Actions, real motives and consequences are relative, just like any other truth in life. Finally, as a result, our history books are the ones written by the winners. The losers most probably have written their side of the story just to see it burned like the big libraries of ancient civilisations.

The Xianyang Library, the Library of Alexandria, the Library of Antioch, the Library of Nalanda, the Grand Library of Baghdad...

Our war was no different, one of the first casualties of the civil war was the Lebanese National Library. According to some sources, some of the most precious manuscripts disappeared.

This is exactly why we ignore so many things about our past. It was either burnt or time slowly dissolved it into nothingness.

Curiosity is considered a sign of strength and one of the main reasons for humanity's superiority over all other life forms; so, if a tree was as curious as we are, it would have recorded the behaviour of animals, humans, the stars and anything that could affect its existence.

Of course, that would represent big troubles to our race's progress. They would have found out how harmful we are to the rest of the planet, then took the right measures to adapt, evolve and defend themselves.

I mean, some trees are thousands of years old which is older than most of our civilisations.

They communicated with each other way before we invented the internet. In fact, a tree in the middle of jungle could know what's happening far, far away, because all trees are connected through a web of roots that go so deep beneath the earth, but still, they choose to keep giving us fruits, shelters and oxygen.

I could only imagine a conversation between some trees living close to the madness of the war.

An exceptionally wise 6000-year-old olive tree advising an old cedar tree and other younger trees by calling for a change, preaching others about ways to fight back and ways to destroy the human race's superiority.

Wise Olive Tree: Wake up you sleepy, lazy bunch of young branches. I've been living for five thousand years, and I've seen all the atrocity of those straight walking creatures.

The wind blowing, carrying its message beyond the seas and the oceans to reach Asia, Europe, the Americas and each and every corner in which there's a living tree.

Younger trees would listen but dare not comment.

Wise Olive Tree: I witnessed the development of that species, from the day they fought using our branches, to them cutting us down to make boats, build fences and furniture.

The trees being so quiet and taking a moment of silence, grieving with patience and pain.

Wise Olive Tree: It's time to take action, time to stop giving those arrogant creatures our gifts.

Other older trees would engage in the conversation.

Older Tree 1: We are too old to fight back.

Older Tree 2: How can we stop giving them fruits? How can we stop exhaling oxygen?

The Cedar Tree, who is 3000 years old, finally speaks up.

Cedar Tree: I have lived up these mountains way before many of you were born; I saw the greed and the ignorance of those creatures, and I saw the forest being reduced to an attraction park…

Taking a short pause as if to gain motivation.

Cedar Tree: I saw them fighting and killing each other in the most unimaginable ways. I fear no storm, no lightning and no animals, but I fear the self-destructive powers of these cursed humans.

Wise Olive Tree: These idiots are confusing curiosity with intelligence. Their philosophers spoke too much and wrote on papers made of our leaves, but they still didn't realise that intelligence is harmony and peace.

The birds nesting on my branches are smart; they fly, build nests, migrate and reproduce, then they die. Worms eaten by those birds have the same journey and purpose.

Cedar Tree: These are the rules of life and we can't change it, the end will come, sooner or later, so why fight it?

Wise Olive Tree: Humans changed those rules, by putting themselves on the top of the chain. They are deciding our future and the future of our beloved earth.

The Wise Olive Tree felt so bad that it held its breath, maybe giving an example in leadership. It slowly died, cause of death: suicide.

The other trees kept on living as if nothing happened.

Did I do the same on the fenceless balcony that day? Was I getting fed up of the war routine and I decided to put an end to my misery? Was it a suicidal action due to the Post-Traumatic Stress Disorder?

PTSD

Post-Traumatic Stress Disorder is obviously a mental health condition caused by traumatic events. And what could be more traumatic than war?

I could see the symptoms on each person living our war, but we all were living in denial, including kids who pretended to be strong and coping with the daily happenings.

I was no different. Just like Venus before me, I went into a coma.

I dived into the unknown trying to escape our sad daily existence, not aware that an entire population was in a coma or a special support system to stay alive. The food and other basic necessities were running scarce; some organisations were distributing bread, food and used clothes…covering school fees and medical fees…without those aids most people would have suffered greatly and probably starved to death…

Only those who were directly involved with the militias had the luxury of not begging for humanitarian aids. The rest had to wait in lines and fill a form after another.

Just like an untreated coma could lead to a persistent vegetative state, the majority of my fellow country citizens were getting numb either by stopping to care or by alcoholism and the use of other drugs. But what was happening to me? Was I becoming a plant?

To avoid the medical terms, I'll put it this way:

A human in a vegetative state is still considered alive but is less than a human being, less than an animal, equal to a plant and barely better than a stone.

Apparently, I never reached the vegetative stage, the coma was short-lived and I snapped out of it before I got to communicate with my fellow trees and plants.

Unlike many other people, I didn't undergo any near death experience: no bright light, no floating above my own body and looking down at it, no passage through a tunnel, no meeting angels or any other superpowers.

I didn't go to Hell, faced no demons and endured no taste of punishment. There wasn't anything bizarre, like travelling out to the universe, to other planets, meeting celebrity figures from the past, going underwater or to a field of flowers…It was just a short journey into emptiness.

It was as vain as the reality surrounding me and as brutal as war. It was unusual to hear of a death not related to the war. Even to this day, when I search back in my memories, I hardly recall anyone who peacefully ceased living. It was either people were too careful to catch critical diseases, or everything was blamed on war.

The story could have been finished at this point. I could have never awakened. The war would have ended for me same as life. Call it a wishful thought, a lucid dream or a temporary ceasefire that lasted twenty-six hours. The illusion was over same as all ceasefires were.

There was no magical erase button of all the war memories, instead, I opened my eyes, scared, confused and convinced of a conspiracy that led to all of this.

To make a long story short, I was back from the emptiness with one unnoticed syndrome, yet to be discovered, called 'paranoia'.

"Paranoia" is a mental illness and not a personality trait, it could be permanent or temporary.

For many years, doctors related this psychological illusion only to humans, just because it was believed that we are the only specie capable of having a complex imagination.

Even if squirrels look always suspicious, move frantically and act paranoid, they are actually rodents in a constant state of prudence from predators…Noises, movements or any sudden incident would trigger an articulation and a behaviour of a paranoid human. In fact, paranoid people look like squirrels and not the contrary.

However, recent observations proved that certain animals such as ravens have paranoid abstract thoughts about their minds. This means, they can actually get paranoid based on illusions, imaginary thoughts and things that only exist in their minds…

These findings were another disappointment of our humanity's ego and self-proclaim of uniqueness.

In all cases, paranoia is usually accompanied by other mental illnesses, such as: depression, dementia, delusional disorder and schizophrenia…

The symptoms can vary from strange behaviours of having imaginary enemies, friends, ghosts, aliens to hearing voices of gods and demons.

Some even go as far as to say that most prophets and saints are schizophrenic and the voices they heard were nothing but the sick echoes of their brain…As soon as I opened my eyes in the emergency room, everything looked different and I struggled to know what was going on.

Everything was so quiet, calm, and peaceful, but there was a terrible smell of sickness. And by that, I do not mean the weird scent of medicines and chemical combinations, nor the usual smell of gunpowder, burning cars and bodies…

The war, life, Heaven and Hell, in fact everything from existential to theoretical concepts became one big interrogation mark.

I opened my eyes with images, flashes and chronicles of the events that I missed the first years of my life. I realised that my story didn't start when the sniper spared my life, and that some of the most horrible incidents happened while I was still an infant learning to lift my head, to listen, to smile and to do my first steps. I remembered the sounds of bombs that became the usual lullabies.

It was all buried deep down in the back of my mind, either by hearing my surrounding talking about it or on the radios and TV.

I must have drawn my own images of those events. They all came back while I was away in that coma; smashed vegetables on the roads, broken furniture, burned wheels mixed with ripped bloody clothes of infants, kids and civilians. I saw my strawberry jam sandwich on the floor, but it was spilling blood. I saw militants getting executed with cold blood. I saw my father carried to the hospital the night I was having my first tooth…He got spared from death but kept a bullet forever lodged behind his kidney.

I lived every massacre that happened nearby during my infant years. I lived the fear, saw the destructions and the atrocities. I heard the cries, the prayers and the begging. I felt the pain, the hatred and misery caused by war…But then I opened my eyes with a single tear.

Were those all nightmares or post-traumatic symptoms?

I wondered why I woke up and started thinking of multiple scenarios about different theories of what really happened to me. Unfortunately, the more a person thinks, the more questions arise, and the more answers are found, the more doubts are raised. I wasn't the only paranoid one though. Symptoms of the war were so common that each person was coming up with a different theory. Conspiracy theories started popping up like popcorn.

Journalists, politicians, investigators and regular citizens were mumbling their own version of a conspiracy theory.

Admitting a mistake is not man's best quality, denying it is easier for the conscience. That's why most of my countrymen were blaming these events on external powers:

– The war being a backstage for the USSR and the USA Cold War. This was definitely the most popular theory.

– Then Zionism came second; separating Judaism from Zionism, and each got its share of the blame.

– The old colonial countries, the Brits and French were teaching us a lesson for taking our independence.

– Of course, religion took a big part of that too. Each sect claimed it was its duty to protect and conquer our holy land.

Amongst the many theories, those were the most logical conspiracies, but there were others that were less compelling.

Like our human's biology; things such as the effect of our cuisine on our tempers and behaviours… Maybe these were the reasons behind all that thirst for war and violence.

DNA, a genetically mismatch error, was making all those people living in the country unable to cohabit.

Aliens, UFOs and extra-terrestrial interference for experimental reasons.

Messing with the economy; controlling the oil industry; taking over our food supply; money laundering.

When each conspiracy stopped making any sense and was proven untrue, intellectuals started combining what was left.

The USA was made up of Zionists and the USSR were still the new colonial communist power; the aliens genetically designing a new DNA; or Mediterranean cuisine taking over the world economy.

The religions and sectarian sides got mixed with economy, food mixed with the oil industry, biology with policies and history with extra-terrestrials.

I remember an old man going around and explaining how God is economy, and how religions have nothing to do with the real Creator.

Most people dismissed him and considered him a lunatic. He always started with the conclusion.

"God is the economy. He is money!"

To prove his point, he would ask questions, but since nobody wanted to answer, he would go on and keep talking.

"Just close your eyes and imagine. When the economy is good, everybody is fine. Some people are workaholics, right?"

Even if no one answered or engaged in the conversation, he wouldn't stop.

"Of course, I'm right! If the economy is good, a workaholic would work and make a fortune. Other people would prefer to work a little and live off of fishing and drinking beer."

Most people didn't want to listen to that old man and he used to get answers like: Leave me alone, I have kids to feed, I have no time for that blasphemy…

"Open your mind and listen! When the economy is good, the little things would make life good enough to live. Just like saying "God is Great." But instead, we say the economy is great and everybody is happy, doing what they like and loving it."

He died in a mysterious way few years later. His body was never found. It truly was a period of bad economy.

As time passed by, the economic war grew stronger, the national currency went weaker, and people lost the value of their money. The population's income and wellness was changing; the middle class were turning poor while new rich were popping up due to the war's benefits and corruption. More people were looking for a better life elsewhere and immigration was the only choice. Day after day, I remembered the words of that old man, whom I considered as a prophet.

The theories grew in numbers and quality on a daily basis as the war collected more lives. I was too young to understand any of the theories, but I always listened and tried to come up with my own conclusions.

The explosions were increasing in numbers and quality. While the war zone was slowly expanding in size and spreading like a vicious cancer. The country was facing a financial disaster, a currency crisis and a total economic collapse.

What used to be a safe haven, turned to a long-term risky investment. But people didn't starve, money wasn't scarce, and no one died out of a lack. Money was coming from somewhere and it kept people under control, numb and ignorant of the atrocity of the

is dreams, his hopes and ambitions were diverted to those of a western living person with different concerns and worries, it was as if he surpassed those traumatic years of war. He couldn't fit back with the environment anymore and only stayed a week then left back with his mom taking with them the middle brother. It was a new kind of mixed immigration.

The forced migration wasn't new at all. Over the centuries, the Jews with the pretext of holy wars were forced by economic and political reasons to leave their land and resettle in different parts of the world. In their turn, the Jewish politicians or Zionists, as I explained earlier, decided to return the favour and considered the Bible as a proof for the ownership of the Promised Land or what is now called Israel. warlords.

A Welcome to Teenage Era

Days, months and years passed, but nothing really changed. As if time stopped and people stopped moving forward, they were stuck in the same nightmare, reliving the same events over and over again. Maybe the events were actually changing, but it seemed that the misery wasn't. The childhood's innocence was gone for good and that little boy I used to be became a teenager.

That new young traumatised man was witnessing a new era: the refugee crisis was getting worse, with few invasions and foreign military interventions. This led to the creation of a new resistance and liberation movements and an increase of the existing ones. Those new rises started bombing invaders and their supporters, and as their precedents, they lost their ways and turned into militias fighting each other.

Political and military measures that aimed to control that crisis proved to deepen the division and to demonstrate no serious intentions to solve nor to end the war. Those same leaders and their parties needed to come up with new strategies to keep the masses scared and always seeking for their protections.

Time flew by so fast and people were still fighting, frontiers were still the same, no one won and no one lost. In a blink of an eye, the world was changing.

I survived the next couple of years maintaining a low profile. No one had the time to notice any unusual symptoms. I spent my days between shelters, hiding my emotions and reading books. Everyone was searching to escape reality in a way or another. Some were playing cards in the refugees, while others were drinking their days and dreaming of an alternative reality. My family, along with many others found comfort in praying to God, hoping that this nightmare will end soon. But the harsh reality was that most of the men were still on the frontiers fighting the unknown enemy.

The guerrilla war was getting fiercer, weapons deadlier and the people were getting traumatized.

Just like everybody else, I became less interested in solving the conspiracies because I was getting affected by the general mood, which was that no one seemed to understand what's going on in this war. So, like most other historians, I lost track of the body counts, the collected souls and the changing rivals.

I think most people especially civilians were getting tired and the new way of surviving became escaping the war zone, giving up on understanding, or to make it crystal clear: it was about living and breathing. The people that refused to think of a life in a different country few years earlier were starting to knock at the embassies' doors begging for visas.

In some cases, a dramatic story or a bad accident could in time, have a nice ending for some people. Such as this story; when in a calm day, a rocket hit a family of five living in the fifth floor in a neighbourhood building. The eldest boy and his dad were not in the house, the middle boy was in his bedroom, and the mom and the youngest boy were in the living room.

For no apparent reason and during a ceasefire period, the building shook with a loud explosion, glass shattered, a sudden silence, then some loud shouting, crying, and people running for help. The rocket had exploded in the living room where my friend and his mom used to pray.

Neighbours entered the house and found the middle boy traumatised in his room, the youngest boy with wounds and blood all over his body, while parts of his mom's body spread all over the room.

They were taken to a near-by hospital; the poor lady was severely injured, while the youngest boy had some minor wounds. The rest of the family were unharmed, but their real pain was emotional because this rocket had broken their souls.

A week later, we never saw them again. A French association took the mom to Paris in order to be hospitalised. They took the young and middle boy, in order to give them a better life and be next to their mom. The rest of the family stayed home and waited.

These were the days were people still didn't want to leave. But everything changed and few years later, the unfortunate kids that used to disappear from school either because something terrible happened to their parents or because they found a foster house somewhere in Europe were considered the lucky ones.

It was at this time of my life, that I started to be aware of the concept of human migration. Even if it was happening inside my country since the start of the war. First came the refugees settling in new areas, then the locals relocated willingly or by force, mostly due to their religions, sects or political beliefs.

The demography of the country was changing faster than the norm, which could only lead to disaster.

The unique cultural mosaic that was formed through thousands of years of interactions with regional powers, settlers, conquerors, invaders and colonialism was shattered in just a few years.

Most people looked at that diversity as a curse that needs to end, but only a minority was persuaded to leave their land, and even when they did, they made sure they didn't leave it for the other party.

Human migration isn't a new thing though, people started moving from one place to another before any civilisation; hunters-gatherers were constantly on the move before settling down in specific areas.

In a way just like some animals have a routinely annual migration that is determined by rain, drought and different weather changes.

There are some amazing journeys done by birds, mammals, reptiles and fish…The most interesting to me are:

Salmon Migration: These fishes decide at a certain time of the year that they are ready to swim from the ocean to the upper reaches of the river, in order to find the exact place in which they started their lives, to spawn on a gravel bed, or simply to give birth to next generations…Once the mission is accomplished, the ones that survived the dangerous exhausting journey, and have nothing left to do but die and give all the nutrients from their decomposing carcasses to the river, the forest and the animals that live in it.

An epic tale of bravery, perseverance, love, dedication and sacrifice.

Penguin Migration: These flightless birds have a similar journey to the salmons; they travel miles and miles from the South Pole to the ocean, taking a different path every year because of shifting ice, and guess for what? To find their nesting place and hatch their eggs in order to give birth and raise their chicks till they are strong enough to take care of themselves and their turn, repeat the same migration patterns of the penguin march of their parents.

Grasshopper Migration: These are some serious insects that have been roaming our planet for about 250 million years; they haven't had the best relationship with humans in any period of history. These insects gather in large groups at certain circumstances and become known as locust…serious devastating pests.

The reason is pure economical, only when there's a shortage of food, they increase in numbers and fly all together without even landing for days, till they find a green area and devour the crops and everything they find on their way, then they move on again…

What brings me back to my story, a locust invaded the land of my forefathers during the First World War and caused a famine and the first major migration to the Americas.

In fact, climate change and the search for food were the main reason for humans' migration, I'm not sure how scientifically accurate our history is, and whether our ancestors truly descended from Africa and left it about two million years ago, then spread all over the planet…or maybe, different races originated in different continents then they interbred and we are the result of it…It's a very sensitive discourse that could lead to racism and human's division. However, the recent migration that peaked in the last 200 years is well recorded and better known as immigration; it's divided into two categories, selected and forced.

Wars, poverty and famine were pushing people in the line of fire to run and find asylum in safer places, and their kids adapted to these new places, and after the third generation, it became difficult to have any attachment to their roots.

My neighbour young friend came back to visit his dad and brother after living in Paris for few years. He was a totally different person. It was as if he wanted to erase that part of the child trauma he lived and I believe that it was a successful detachment operation. The look, the attitude, the interests and the humour had all changed to a typical French kid.

A drastic demographic was happening on a very high level. And unlike the animal's kingdom, this was an unnatural migration. In fact, it was:

"The deeds for the lands from God directly were an excuse good enough to force the people living in that area to flee their homes and resettle in other countries…"

Creating a refugee crisis and destabilising many other countries including mine. However, in recent history, this happened in many other regions like Africa, the Balkans, the Indian Peninsula, the Americas and others…

I was living the consequences of history lessons in the During my puberty. People's physical and psychological symptoms worsened enormously during that period. It added more confusion to a situation that was already reaching an extreme. Some people were still dying. Many were

immigrating as the rest quietly watched the events, wondering
what's next.

Changes

All these events stopped mattering, as if the bombs, death and destruction became meaningless and the repetition opened my eyes to the side effects. Suddenly, the emotional side of the war was becoming the main story.

We were all getting traumatised and that's a fact. No matter if people lived in the most affected areas such as my neighbourhood or other villages and cities that were far from the regular war zones, the tide reached every single soul in a way or another.

The real question to me was: Does these mental disorders heal with time? Does it get into DNA? Will we ever have a normal life? Did the young friend that escaped the country got really over those horrendous past images and fears?

I had no idea what to believe and what to make out of all the confusing events. Wars tend to turn people more religious. They all have a godly sponsor, praying, donating money and dying in the name of God becomes more frequent.

The irony is that in a civil war, opposite parties praying for their spiritual leaders are actually submitting the same request: victory, safety for their families, end of war and peace.

It would be very simple and easy if the party that loses admits that their god either abandoned them, or that the other god is more powerful. However, humans always find excuses: God has other plans, he was testing their faith, he needed more prayer and commitment, we didn't deserve his help, or that he doesn't interfere in wars…

In that specific case, what complicated the matter even more is that nobody won. A stalemate was the end result.

Everybody was getting sick of this tragedy, but nobody was willing to renounce any religion.

The alternative was looking for a human saviour, a messenger from the gods who could change the situation and put an end to the madness.

After all, we lived on the ancient lands of the Canaan, where Phoenician gods were worshipped for centuries, then the Greek gods and the Roman ones. But none of the gods interfered directly in human wars. They sent messengers and gave emotional and psychological support.

The most successful leaders through history claimed that divine intervention got them into leadership positions. That's how they made the masses praise them, fight for them and die or them. By using the oldest trick in history, enhance the feelings and promise change.

I was only thirteen years old when the country ended without a president, a divided army and many equally strong militias. Life was becoming uninteresting and death was considered a blessing; it seemed to everybody that nothing will ever change.

Any storyteller or filmmaker could see traits of a melodrama. Something needed to be done, a refresh, a shuffle or a new twist in the tale.

I like to believe that the gods of wars were losing followers, ratings and viewers. A change was inevitable. How could a screenwriter turn a lame script into an award winning one?

Human's long observation on storytelling assures that people are drawn to the unusual, the unexpected and the mind-blowing.

At that time in which my neighbourhood was getting poorer, the basic human rights of having water, electricity and food were diminishing; the unimaginable happened. A ray of light appeared in the darkness. Out of a sudden, a new character appeared, more than a hero and less than a saviour. There was a hope for an end or a new start.

Meanwhile I was not a kid anymore and I was so unconcerned about the entire events, the story took the form of a comic strip.

A leader in charge, a special one or a Centaur 'half civilian and half commander' popped up.

How did that happen?

Very simple, the Cold War was reaching its end. Smaller civil wars were getting fewer attentions, less weapons and money. Other aids became scarce. For all those reasons, the Parliament couldn't meet.

In fact, the Parliament speakers couldn't and wouldn't agree on electing a successor. Therefore, the president appointed the commander-in-chief as acting head of government.

Nice twist, no? It was a nice cocktail, sweet and sour or Ying and Yang. This development brought a change but also added more divisions.

The new leader in charge appealed to the old people who had nostalgia to the old days of peace, to the civilians who were fed up with the war misery and the youth who longed for a better life.

He gained the sympathy and support of a big chunk of the population. He did it by expressing and demonstrating his tough love, patriotism, social boldness and confidence of steel. Considered as a demigod, he had the sight of an eagle and his words were like thunder.

A local modern day Thor! It's said that history repeats itself, a myth does that too. Our new hero promised the end of war, divisions and external interventions. Same as Thor promised to the end Frost Giants.

With the love and support of the people, a relatively small army and his strong will, he waged war against everybody. Even though, he had control of only part of the country shared with many other militias and an occupied area by two neighbouring strong armies. He had no fear and was convinced that rightness will win at the end no matter what.

I remember a very short period of calm and ceasefire; it was the calm before the storm. Everybody was observing patiently.

Conspiracy theories were falling one after the other just like leaves in autumn. Thor invited civilians to his palace, 'a thing never seen before'.

Was it a non-militant movement? A peaceful protest? A civilian disobedience? A carnival or a circus?

For the first time in my life, it wasn't the bombs that stopped us from going to school. Instead, teachers, parents and students voluntarily preferred going to protest and show the world their support to Thor. But when the world turned a blind eye on that scene, the leader started a war with the giant next door.

The army started bombarding the occupying forces and its allies. The favour was returned in double and we spent so many days in the shelters underground playing board games instead of going to school.

There was lots of destruction in my area and casualties, but nobody cared, it was a liberation war and people were more than happy to pay the price. The young men were willing to die in order to liberate the occupied parts of the country and throw out the occupiers.

Of course, that was just an illusion and what years of fighting didn't achieve, neither Thor nor all his ambitions could.

Therefore, the surviving Parliament speakers gathered abroad under international supervision and came up with a new treaty and reforms.

Of course, the commander didn't accept it and dismissed the Parliament. Soon after, they elected a new president, and for the first time in our history, the country ended not only with more than one army but with two presidents too.

There was a lot of anger and disappointment from the United Nations and feeling of betrayal from the Parliament speakers and the world.

The demonstration resumed and this time with a hysterical new look. Chants, slogans, poets and artists were expressing their support to the rightness of the leader and the cause.

It's around that time that we started having blockade on food supply, fuel, electricity and other basic human needs.

But nobody cared, and in a blink of an eye, the country turned into an effervescent bubbly drink, sparkling, fizzy and full of energy, but it all died off quickly.

The older generations were supporting the movement, mothers were sending their kids to join the fight, fathers were dropping the idea of immigration, and the youth were chanting patriotic songs. It turned into an atmosphere of hysteria and joy, sending everybody marching on the streets, protesting, addressing their message to the world. It was all covered by TV stations, radio channels and newspapers, making it an unconventional story stuffed with emotions and heroism.

It was a truly colourful festival on the streets, with fireworks at the beach, which were actually bombs shooting at the ships importing products or delivering fuel. I remember watching the bombs falling in the sea as the ships tried to get closer to the shore.

The audio and visual effects were so realistic that even the famous Cirque du Soleil couldn't compete.

The bombs scared the ships but didn't scare the crowd who were sitting on the shore, sipping their drinks and enjoying the show.

With all that fuzziness around, we could only forget about the tragedies and focus on the positive vibes.

Like the rest of my generation, I was skipping school to go to the beach or even to join a demonstration.

The mighty commander had to come up with a new plan or a new war.

There was no point in resuming the war against the giants, so he looked around and found just one potential opponent 'the bitter ally'.

In a way from all the militias and the armies in that divided little country, he could only raise a war against the strong militia sharing and ruling the same area in which I lived in. This time, it wasn't just a coup, it was one of the fiercest civil war that the country had ever witnessed.

Over the years, this militia became so well armed then it got considered as strong as the National Army and better organised and equipped. This new war was so unexpected and original, as if the screenwriter added a war between Thor and Hercules, or a cage ring fight between Superman and Spiderman. The pretext of this war was not liberation but unifying strength. Two superheroes could not operate in the same area.

Even at that early age, I had no respect for any of the two leaders, but it was that period that each wanted to flex his muscles and there were calls for huge civil protests from the two sides, sometimes a street or two away from each other. I and all schoolmates took that opportunity to skip school and join all protests, sometimes even both on the same day.

Observers and statistician were confused; it appeared as if Thor has 60% of the support while his rival Hercules had 60% too.

Could it be that they were the same schizophrenic 60%?

Schizophrenia is a mental disease worse than the grandiose delusion of the leaders fighting. It seemed as if the entire population was severely diagnosed with it.

Since our history books could never be fair, I have to confess that they were both looking to appeal as the nation's heroes, and people had very little opinion on whom to believe.

No human who is capable of leading a war could be free of what's known as the symptom of greatness. Someone with such ambition and self-confidence could only consider people as numbers and casualties, steps in a stairway that leads to the supreme goal.

It's that damn immortality dream that was passed to us from generation to generation. We can't seem to get over it, no matter how fast we advanced philosophically, scientifically or technologically.

It didn't take long before the inevitable happened; Thor decided to do, as he called it, 'an internal house cleaning'.

A fierce fight started between the two sides that were actually few metres away from each other in each city. There was no way of having the classical wars we had before, instead it turned into a guerrilla war happening from house to house.

Unfortunately, war played on in my neighbourhood. The years of civil war suddenly added more divisions. Neighbours, cousins, friends and even brothers found themselves fighting each other from their house windows and balconies.

This period must have been the worst of them all, or maybe I was just old enough to remember it more. Days and nights spent in shelters with no electricity, no food and no water. People broke into small shops and took whatever they found, but even that was not enough. We had to drink whatever was left in the building's water tank. Later that year, I volunteered to clean it because it was already empty but buzzing with communities of insects, worms and rats. Things started getting even worse and dead people were left for days and weeks in their apartments to rot and stink because no medical support would take the risk of driving an ambulance.

We had no choice but to leave the war zone; the only way this time was by driving through land mines.

It was a game of Russian roulette and we played it to the end. My mom packed as little clothes as possible and we headed to safety. The overpriced taxi trip passed the snipers. The driver told us to put our heads down as he waved a white flag from his window. Out of curiosity, I was turning my neck looking up from the back window, thinking of all the snipers of the other side that I crossed in my life and wondering if those snipers would be any different, as brutal or as merciful.

First stage was successfully completed. There were no bullets shot towards us, but then the car had to drive through the land bombs and the debris of exploded cars. I looked at my mother, she was looking down at her knees, mumbling with prayers. My sister on the other side was staring from the window that looked better than the TV screens of those days. I was observing silently everybody and could notice the different emotions in the car. I remember the driver's poker face and that mixed feeling of hopelessness and emptiness.

Inside my brain, questions and stories formulated. I asked myself: What if I was in that exploded car?

Did the people survive the bomb?

Did they get barbecued alive just like witches and saints in the Middle Ages? Did anyone survive with severe wounds?

Could our car be next?

Could this be the end of life for me?

Unfortunately, I had no answers and that gave me a strange uncomfortable feeling mixed with neither courage, nor fear. There were no tears and no prayers. Just like any Russian roulette participant, there were lots of emotions, hesitation and carelessness.

Maybe this is what years of wars and distress made out of me: 'A vampire, a dead man walking who's not scared of bullets and bombs, instead, scared of light, joy and hope.'

It was only a few kilometres that separated us from the relatively safer part and we made it. Few days later, Thor liberated my neighbourhood from the villain militia that protected it all the past few years.

But that was the only achievement before reaching another stalemate.

There was a division in an already divided small area. Unlike the last time, it was impossible to separate it with containers and sand bags. The area was already so small and entangled by streets, neighbourhoods and people.

The exhausted militia found itself in a lose-lose situation: giving up to Thor or join the rest of the world in accepting the other elected government on the other side of the country. It was like choosing between suicide and slow death.

In the meanwhile, the wind was blowing changes in the world; the countdown for the end of the USSR and the Cold War was getting closer, no one cared about the small war on our little piece of land anymore.

Bigger nations had bigger plans now and just like that the once strong militia chose slow death instead of an irreversible suicide. Thor was facing the entire planet. He had no ally and no friends. His exhausted army and the people were still ready to sacrifice their lives for him. Same as a human would crush an ant colony to clean up a mess, the green light for a full invasion was given. In just few hours, the airplanes filled the skies, airstrikes bombed all the military key defence areas with great accuracy and success. All kind of telecommunication was interrupted. Many soldiers gave up their lives on the battlefield thinking that they could not lose that war and their commander, believing myths of patriotism, bravery and self-sacrifice. The fortress was totally invaded, but Thor had the time to escape and get asylum while many of his faithful followers got executed, kidnapped or just vanished. The next few days were filled with anxiety and confusion; the takeover was totally announced and it became clear for everybody that the illusion of a war that no one could win was a big lie, 'a comedy'.

Opposing leaders were assassinated; the new president went to the old evacuated palace, the remaining soldiers of the weakened army unified with the other army. Then the exiled leaders came back to power as heroes of the moment and the saviour of the future. New political faces appeared, a new era started and a new government was getting ready to rebuild that country and erase all marks of the civil war. The last obstacle had to be removed. The slow death the militia chose was getting closer; at first, it got disarmed, transformed into a political party and then its leader was imprisoned for treason and murder. It ended by getting the party classified as banned.

It was such a perfect blank page to start a new chapter.

Human rights and all nations turned a blind eye on the atrocity of the change. It was a price that the word had to pay for ending that long fabricated civil war.

The Charade

More than fifteen years had passed since the start of the war; the result was more hatred and more divisions.

An entire generation was born in a state of war. Peace for them was more of a bedtime fairy tale. It was a generation with no real understanding of the country concept and the nationalism values. It was a generation with more loyalty to political parties, sects and religious leaders than the whole entity.

Was it because of the family education? The religious influence? The society's structure? Or was it caused by all the inherited mental disorders?

The values were changed and it was so difficult to put things back in a natural order. There were no magic wands and no wizards of love to miraculously undo the damage.

People needed to forget and life needed to go on, so politicians did what politicians do. They came up with slogans, campaigns of forgiveness and reconciliation. Positive vibes were filling the atmosphere, and everybody wanted to believe that the nightmare was over.

It was the start of a game, a new season from a TV series or a book with new plot. The characters remained the same but by flipping a page, a new chapter started, with a new start, a happier one, a funnier or more adventurous one.

Was it a spaghetti western movie? Scenes of decapitated body parts, heads flying and blood splashing all over… Exaggerated violence that makes the entire scene so funny…Or was it a dark comedy that mixed reality drama and pain with a pinch of humour…Putting a smile on the face of the viewer but combining it with disgust and anger.

Was it an open-ended book? The kind of ending that could have multiple interpretations and none could be dismissed as false.

I had no idea how and why, but suddenly they started removing the containers, the sandbags and all other barriers, the frontiers were physically removed. Unconsciously, those frontiers were still there and people from both sides had doubts every time they cross them.

It was so surreal to actually walk on the same streets and not have a visual obstacle. It felt unnatural to see the other side without running or hiding. It felt like waking up from a nightmare, hazed and confused. The questions started rushing in:

Is this real?

Was I dreaming? Am I still dreaming? Where Am I?

What day is it? Which year is it?

Am I still alive and why?

Is it a trick and the enemy will try to ambush us if we cross that imaginary border?

People tried to avoid talking or thinking about the issue, I did the same. But walking in front of the destroyed buildings made me wonder about the snipers:

What happened to them?

Did they go back to their families?

Do they have regrets? Are they living in guilt for taking innocent lives? Or feeling proud of their actions and contribution in the war?

Is there still a sniper hiding his rifle and his weapons, refusing to let go his life, his past and his present?

Walking on some streets was causing strange reactions:

I could see people's heads were turning in all directions; their eyes were filled with fear as if they were analysing the surrounding. I could imagine that just like me, their ears were humming with the sound of bombs and machine guns, while the hearts were accelerating in a frantic way.

How could a dream feel so real? What's going on?

Was it a collective dream or some kind of unexplained reality?

For other people, it was like waking up with a hangover, dizzy, funny and puzzled. Most memories and events were gone and only the physical ache remained. Waking up after so many years of a civil war with just hangover's symptoms!!! What a beautiful way to start a new day. The only way to describe it is by glorifying the grace of forgetfulness. And it's not due to aging but due to young irresponsible boozing. Alcohol must be the modern public enemy of all nations, but it's interesting to know that it's nature's survival of the fittest law that made us the descendants of those first humans who had more tolerance to alcohol.

Let me put it this way; our ancestors were hunters-gatherers, whenever they couldn't hunt or pick up the fruits, they gathered the old fruits that fell from the trees and fermented naturally on the ground…

Those who were not alcohol tolerant got drunk and got eaten by predators, got into fatal accidents or starved to death…

No wonder, people consume more alcohol during war in particular and hard times in general, and no wonder, my generation's appetite for alcohol was so high. It didn't take long to wake up from that hangover though and start remembering the awful truth. When my countrymen woke up with that new barrier-less reality, it wasn't easy to look at the other side without feeling the fear, the anger and that bitter disgusting aftertaste in their throats.

It was impossible to forget the lost ones, the sacrifices and all the hatred. However, politicians who stayed in charge started running the newly reunited country, promoting their new vision of a better nation, filling the head of the people with positive propaganda and dreams.

People started visiting the other side, checking their abandoned houses, their villages and the leftovers of their lost memories. Nothing was the same though, just like a broken vase, the scars couldn't heal.

An entire population decided to live in denial instead of facing the facts. I heard the people talking about hope and a glorious future compared to the near past that happened before the fall and breaking the vase. Now I realise that neither me nor the politicians new about the Japanese philosophy 'wabi-sabi'.

Wabi-Sabi

I learned years later that the politicians' promises and plans for people's safe return to the villages they fled during the war, the rebuild of the destroyed country and its infrastructure and most of all, the oath of 'forgiveness and peace' was nothing valuable. It was nothing but words travelling in the vast universe.

The country, the politicians and the people were divided, incompatible and broken. A nation severely affected with anxiety and multiple mental and psychological disorders.

How could a broken vase be fixed?

How could anyone delete the past and forget? Is forgiveness a holy virtue or a cowardly act?

Would a time machine solve the problem and let the people who fought on both sides resign from repeating the same mistakes?

Would a divine intervention prevent those 15 years from happening?

Politicians seemed very sure that they were not to be blamed, that none of them lost and none of them won. It was a confusing period for those who were trying to understand the next step or go on with their lives.

It took us time to get used to the new characters calling the shots, to the new plans of reform, rebuilding and reuniting the nation. Most people, including myself, had big hopes of a better future. After all, the physical barriers were removed from the streets but graver ones replaced them in people's minds.

Out of a sudden, a genius idea of rebuilding the capital as a priority appeared. Since the 5000 years old capital was almost totally destroyed and most people who owned the properties couldn't afford to rebuild, the government approved creating a real estate company that forced everybody to give their property in return of shares. It was the first sign of twisting democracy into a masked dictatorship and the most corrupted regime that ever existed.

To be fair to my beloved city, I need to give few historical facts:

Beirut, one of the oldest inhabited cities, more than 5000 years of history, destroyed and rebuilt seven times 'mostly by invaders and earthquakes'.

It's considered as a rich world heritage…By the end of the civil war, the city was turned into a ghost city.

The army took possession of the 'downtown'.

The main objective of the politicians was to restore that ancient city, and in fact, modern archaeology had the best chance to dig under its ruins and find many of its lost stories…The finds were fantastic, but politicians had no time to waste on the past no matter how far it was…The rebuilding process covered destroyed and bulldozed many of its underneath archaeological discoveries.

They replaced Canaanite City walls, crusaders fortress walls, Iron Age shaft tombs and many complete well reserved mosaics with spaces for parking lots and shopping centres.

Part of the country's past has been lost forever. Few people had access to the construction sites and no records were kept of the looting…The old city was totally taken over and renovated. It looked like a copy of an old city, a fake version of what was once the pearl of the Middle-East had risen.

I wish the country, the people and mostly the politicians were mature enough to embrace the imperfect as the practitioners of Wabi-sabi do.

Some damage could never be undone. A broken heart can forgive but never forget. Wabi-sabi tells us that the best thing to do with a broken vase is to put it back together without trying to hide the marks of the past.

Without covering the scars with makeup, concealers, nor even aesthetic surgeries. Letting the wrinkles tell their stories…building around the debris and scattered pieces as a reminder for future generations.

This was not what most of the politicians thought and those who disagreed were ignored or silenced.

Instead the parliament voted for a modern country with modern cities, the materialistic era, the bling-bling, the quick profit, the corruption. All those shaped the new version of the failed nation.

It must have been around that time which I was convinced that I can't call this place and this land home.

Many parents started sending their kids abroad, a new wave of immigration. My frustration wasn't much different, so I considered gypsy hood as a more sophisticated lifestyle form.

Minimalism, freedom, having no belongings other than the air, the mountains and oceans was inspiring my soul and I decided to leave.

From that day, I lost hope in my country, in its political system and its population. I packed my suitcase with clothes, a camera and some books, then I took an airplane and left to the first destination I could.

Time passed, almost as quickly as the war. I lived in Europe, North America and the Arabian Peninsula.

I travelled and wandered around many parts of the world with a hope of never coming back to my traumatic birthplace.

With every experience lived and passing second, I convinced myself that I found peace with myself and my traumas.

I watched from far the atrocities of the political scenes of an endless new way of war. I followed on the media the assassinations, the massacres and the suppression of an entire population. I witnessed a regime metamorphosing from bad to worst. I got shocked with unexpected events, such as exiled and imprisoned war criminals coming back to the new political life. I observed invasions and ferocious wars…However, I alienated myself and buried my head in the ground. I lived in denial, saying that whatever happening is not concerning me, that no geographic borders define me and that I'm a gypsy soul of the universe.

Only after thirty-five years from the day the sniper spared me did I come back, in the country that was supposedly my home. I came with my wife and my two-year-old son.

We thought it would be nice to get him some memories before leaving the country for good.

Again, and again, I was shown that life is full of surprises. The only realistic plan is no plan.

A few months later, we received an email: 'Your application has been cancelled.'

The reason was a corrupted file, the translation of my son's birth certificate. The lawyer informed us about this news with great disturbance and told us that it's one of those unusual events.

There was the denial stage and we tried to complain, reach the officials for reconsideration of our case, but the answer was the same: 'The application has been cancelled and you can always try again.'

The modern civilised world is too hypocritical to admit it. I wish it was a fair world and I didn't have to continue this vicious circle of traumatic childhood.

Canada the land of the…whatever…just decided that we were not good enough to get a normal life away from 'home'.

History repeats itself…'for idiots', for people and societies that don't learn from their past mistakes. I felt unconcerned, but it took a couple of years to find myself and my family trapped. Just like my father and my grandfather before him, the country plunged in revolutions. And just like me, my four-year-old son held the flag and went to the streets asking for political reforms. It was like a remake of a classic old movie. However, this time it was even greater. But I accepted my situation, imagining that nothing worse could ever happen in this era. I was wrong and the calls for changes lead to more political divisions, resignations and disastrous economic crisis.

The Apocalyptic End

What more could happen to an entity at the bottom of a hole? A total system collapse? A label of a failed state? Another sectarian clash? A civil war? A military invasion? Nothing we haven't seen and lived before, right? I tried to put my youth traumas on the side and stay positive.

I admit it, I was totally wrong, the situation escalated, the protests turned into confrontations between the citizen and the army. Streets were blocked and people took over the main streets in the major squares in the cities. Banks took that as an excuse and decided that it's not safe to open any branches, which was the first move into capturing people's savings.

As the government stepped down, the demonstrations turned more violent and people got more frustrated.

And as if it wasn't bad enough, a pandemic broke through the world and spread in an uncontrollable speed. People were kicked out of the streets and forced to stay at home. Airports shut down and an entire population got imprisoned. A total lockdown gave a new elected government some extra time to make new deals and find ways to hide their years of failure.

While people were begging the banks to release their money, the local currency gradually started going down, until it lost 85 to 90 percent of its value. There were different exchange rates and ways for the banks to rip off the people's savings whether it's in local currency or US dollars.

An entire population ended up broke and rubbed by its political leaders.

A new generation of kids was having online and home schooling, others were seeing their parents complaining, jobless and unable to provide their minimum needs.

Hope is a strange humane act, isn't it? It's an illusion that leads to more traumas and failures. My countrymen and women kept hoping, so did I.

I knew that every story comes to an end, but I was getting so numb and careless. I lived day by day as an observer waiting for a boom, and unfortunately, I didn't have to wait for long.

In a routinely summer day, I got into my car to go see old friends in my childhood neighbourhood where everything started, where I was born and where I saw the first ray of light accompanied with the sounds of bombs. The 30-minute drive took more than two hours due to traffic caused by the army and special anti-riots forces that blocked roads to stop a small number of protesters from freely reaching some areas. Since life was going on a slow motion, I didn't turn back and took the longer road passing through the heart of Beirut. I remember that strange spooky feeling mixed with anxiety and a worrying feeling in the stomach. As my car was moving really slowly, I couldn't stop from wondering what's next; I looked at my left side and saw some of the old houses that haven't been renovated yet mixed with modern towers…I looked and somehow felt sorrow.

So I turned my head to the right side, where the seaport silos and wondered what's the future hiding for that city? And then, that slow mood faded down and I started my irresponsible drive track; within few minutes of breaking some rules, cutting other cars, going wrong way and passing red lights…and in that haze of reality, I found myself with a beer in my hand and talking to my old friends in my childhood neighbourhood. It was like if this was all I needed from life, like if I discovered the simple secret of happiness.

Then we heard a boom…what the fuck? Very little time to react, just scared faces and wondering eyes…Then a big explosion was heard, a door flew from the second floor's balcony and hit a car next to mine, shattered glasses started raining down…

It's war…we are getting bombed…hide inside I heard.

I thought that it was the end, and just like Paulo Coelho's *The Alchemist*, my story will end in the same place it started, but instead of finding the treasure I wandered to find, I'd find death.

I jumped in my car without even saying bye or checking on anyone…I need to get home I thought…check on my loved ones and get back to my bed…I left so fast with a beer still in my hand, an act of cowardness or an instinct of survival…I really can't tell.

However, driving back home was an apocalyptic ride, shattered glasses all over, people standing on the streets next to their broken shops wondering what the hell happened… shattered glasses everywhere… cars on the roads driving with a panic mode…

Then I raised my head up to sip my beer and I saw an orange cloud covering the sky. I kept driving a little faster, thinking that I'm getting away from the blast area, but instead, I was getting closer and was noticing more distraction, cars that looked like smashed tomatoes, buildings with no windows and broken balconies…

I imagined multiple scenarios of a new war with modern biological, chemical or nuclear weapons.

Later that day, after a surrealistic car ride that reminded me of that taxi ride through the land bombs that I realised a huge explosion had happened at the seaport few minutes after I had passed it.

An explosion that was considered the third biggest in all time, the casualties were enormous.

I still don't know if I was lucky to miss that bomb or unlucky to extend my years of suffering in that life.

That night, I couldn't sleep, cheating death hunted me; it could have been me; it could have been my child, my wife, my mother, my cousin…it could have been anyone. If I only took that stop I thought about, if I respected the traffic rules and didn't drive like a maniac, if I stopped to buy a drink or fill my gas tank…so many other ifs…I felt broke, lost and wished I was unreal and wrote:

My heart is aching.

All around, people are weeping,

Whining, crying and grieving.

Economic crises, pandemic spread and explosions,

Wounds, injuries, anger, hate and fear,

Mixed emotions, nothing is clear,

Shattered glasses, rubbles and destructions…

Memories of traumatic civil war revived.

We are doomed to genetically pass those traumas to our kids. As if it's not enough, we're letting them grow with their own new ones. From all the stories of pain, suffering and misery, there's one that marked me like no other.

I heard a mother who lost her child say, "I'll never bring another innocent being in this country…" She had sorrow in her voice and dry tears in her eyes. I felt her pain and identified with her. This place is only suitable for monsters. The traumas that my generation and I lived were supposed to slowly fade and heal with time; instead, it got aggravated and the political leaders threw gas on the fire.

A generation after another created a traumatised society, a whole nation unable to imagine living in peace or cohabitate with itself. On the individual aspect, everybody was suffering from chronic trauma, the symptoms were so noticeable: edgy attitude, living on the edge, materialism and no trust in a higher power or rules…

No therapies and no years of self-improvement would be able to erase those traits.